BIBLICAL BULLETIN BOARDS FOR CHILDREN TO MAKE

by
Anita Reith Stohs

illustrated by Corbin Hillam

Cover by Ted Warren

ISBN No. 1-56417-002-0
Standardized Subject Code TA ac
Printing No. 987654321

Shining Star Publications
1204 Buchanan St., Box 299
Carthage, IL 62321-0299

Unless otherwise indicated, the New International Version of the Bible was used in preparing the activities in this book.

TABLE OF CONTENTS

DEDICATION

To Irene, Miriam, and Daniel Reith
Revelation 22:21

TO THE TEACHER/PARENT

The bulletin board activities in this book have been chosen to illustrate stories from the Old and New Testaments. The individual projects are intended to be visual reminders to students as well as witnesses to other observers. Much of what we learn comes through seeing. These bulletin boards will serve as extremely effective resources for teaching the Bible to your students and congregation.

We also learn by doing. Because involving children in the process of creation can enhance learning, the bulletin boards described in this book all encourage student participation. Encourage your students to help as much as possible as you put together the bulletin boards in your classroom. When you can, include children in teacher preparation activities such as cutting out letters. When alternative ways to make the bulletin boards are presented, involve the children in the decision-making process in choosing an option to follow.

Making class bulletin boards will provide excellent opportunities for children to work together in a positive setting. Assign different tasks to each student, depending upon his abilities. Always find something to praise about each child's efforts. Be careful to accept what each one does as a valid art expression reflecting his individual developmental level. Encourage harmony, not competition, and an appreciation of the contribution made by each member of the class. In this way children will be learning to work peaceably together as part of the "family of God."

The bulletin board patterns and designs found in this book were created to be a springboard. Modify and adapt them as you wish. Be creative with your bulletin boards, and encourage the same quality in the children you teach. Let the techniques described in this book be stepping-stones to your own, unique bulletin board creations in years to come.

SUGGESTIONS FOR MAKING BULLETIN BOARDS

Backgrounds
Experiment with these different kinds of materials for backgrounds:

Shelf paper
Fingerprinted paper
Spatter-painted paper
Typing paper
Construction paper
Tissue paper
Newspaper
Wrapping paper

Poster board
Cardboard
Corrugated cardboard
Wallpaper
Road maps
Magazine pages
Burlap
Felt

Cotton fabric
Corduroy
Flannel
Polyester blends
Netting
Cellophane
Foil

Borders
Decorative edging can be bought from a school supply store or made by cutting strips of paper. For faster cutting, staple several strips together; then cut them at one time.

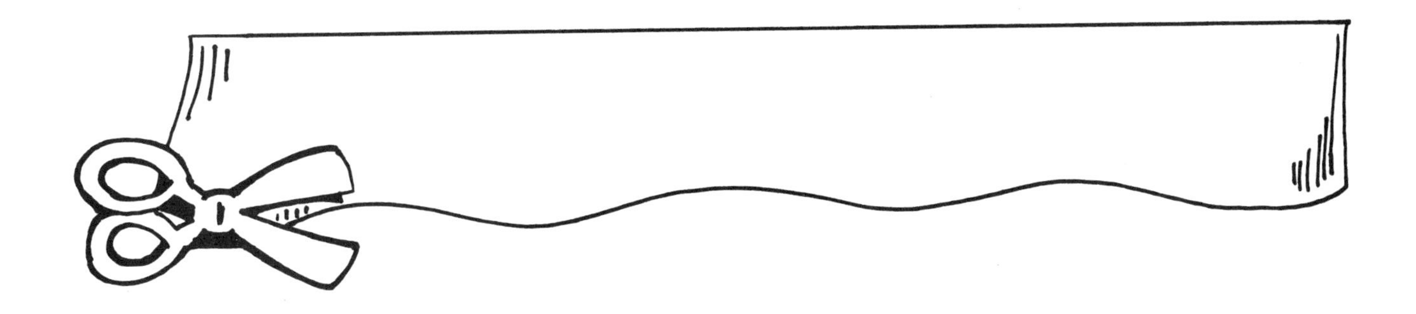

Experiment with other ways to create paper borders. Paper may be looped in various designs, stamped, folded for cutouts, or made into paper chains or corners. Yarn or ribbon can also be used.

Lettering

Letters for bulletin board titles can be cut from any of the materials suggested for backgrounds.

Draw Letters with

Markers
Crayons
Paint
Glitter glue
Colored glue
Chalk dipped in sugar water

Outline Letters with

Wire
Sticks
Ribbon
Toothpicks
Chenille stems
Twisted crepe or tissue paper
Macaroni soaked in cold water
String
Yarn
Straws

Three-Dimensional Bulletin Boards

For a three-dimensional effect, add lightweight objects to your bulletin board. Use balloons, boxes, bags, paper cups, tubes, stuffed paper, and folded paper to add depth.

Letter Patterns

Commercial letters are available to attach to the bulletin board. Cardboard stencils may be used for tracing or spray painting. Letters that may be traced are included on page 96 of this book.

Enlarging Patterns

Use an overhead projector to enlarge figures or letters for the bulletin board. Trace the design you wish to enlarge on a sheet of acetate; then project the design onto a piece of paper taped to the wall. Trace over the projected lines, then color or paint them, or use them as patterns to cut from sheets of colored paper.

General Guidelines

1. Use the bulletin board as a way to emphasize the main lesson of a Bible story.
2. Start with the point you wish to emphasize; choose the illustrations and materials to fit this main point.
3. Keep captions brief; avoid too many words.
4. Look at advertisements in stores and magazines for display techniques you can adapt to fit a biblical theme.
5. Attach the pieces of the bulletin board carefully, hiding pins and staples whenever possible.
6. Change bulletin boards frequently.
7. Create your bulletin boards from a variety of interesting materials.
8. Involve all your students in the creation of the bulletin boards.
9. Encourage cooperative learning in your classroom by dividing the work among the children.
10. Develop a file of bulletin board materials that can be used again.

OLD TESTAMENT

GOD MADE OUR WORLD

Bible Story

Creation of the world. Genesis 1:1

Materials

Blue paper
Nature pictures from magazines
Scissors
Glue
Pencil
String

Teacher Preparation

1. Attach blue paper to the bulletin board.
2. Provide magazines, glue, and scissors.
3. Tie string to pencil.

Classroom Activity

1. Have one child hold one end of the string in the center of the board while another draws a large circle with the pencil.
2. Cut or tear pictures of nature from magazines.
3. Glue the pictures collage style over the circle, trimming them to fit.
4. Cut letters from magazine pictures to create the title "God Made Our World." Glue them on paper. God made a wonderful planet for us to live on. Ask: What place do you like best in this world, and why?

Other Ideas

1. Draw individual pictures of God's world to fit into the circle.
2. Fill in circle with pieces of colored construction or tissue paper.
3. Paint a circle cut from white paper with a watercolor wash.

IN THE BEGINNING

Bible Story

Creation of the world. Genesis 1:1–2:2

Materials

White paper
Crayons or markers
Scissors

Teacher Preparation

1. Cut paper to fit bulletin board.
2. Provide drawing materials and scissors.

Classroom Activity

1. Draw six lines to divide the paper into six puzzle pieces. Cut them out.
2. Outline each puzzle piece with black. Write "Day 1" on one piece, "Day 2" on the second piece, continuing the sequence through "Day 6."
3. Have each child or group of children illustrate a day of creation on a puzzle piece.
4. Each piece should also include a sentence telling what God created on the day illustrated.
5. Put the pieces together on the bulletin board. Talk about how the different parts of God's world fit together to make it "very good."

Other Ideas

1. Draw a large circle to divide into puzzle pieces.
2. Omit the sentence, using only the picture to illustrate each day of creation on the puzzle pieces.
3. Paint pictures with watercolor or tempera.

GOD'S WORLD OF NATURE

Bible Story

Creation of nature. Genesis 1:9-25

Materials

Paper bags
Found nature objects
White paper
Crayons
Scissors

Teacher Preparation

1. Cut paper to fit bulletin board.
2. Provide paper bags and crayons.

Classroom Activity

1. Give each child a paper bag to fill with nature objects such as plants, feathers, rocks, shells, and bark. Go outside and look especially for objects with texture. Have each child talk about what she found. Discuss how God made the different objects for His world.
2. Place some of the nature objects under the paper and rub over them with a crayon. Use different colors of crayons and continue the rubbings until the whole paper is covered.
3. Use a crayon to title the board "God's World of Nature."
4. Attach the paper to the bulletin board.

Other Ideas

1. Glue lightweight nature objects to the bulletin board, using poster board instead of paper.
2. Outline the words for the title with sticks or stones or other natural objects.
3. Make rubbings of specific objects native to the area in which you live, such as seashells or wildflowers.
4. Do rubbings on separate sheets, cut them out, and attach them to the bulletin board in a quilt fashion.
5. Use colored construction paper for individual rubbings.

BLOOM FOR THE LORD

Bible Story

God creates plant life. Genesis 1:9-13

Materials

White paper
Construction paper
Scissors
Pencils

Teacher Preparation

1. Attach white paper to bulletin board.
2. Cut construction paper into squares or rectangles for flowers.
3. Cut construction paper letters for the title "Bloom for the Lord."

Classroom Activity

1. Attach the title, "Bloom for the Lord," to the bulletin board.
2. Think about the many beautiful flowers God put into our world. Choose several to make.
3. Cut symmetrical flowers according to the following directions:
   a. Fold construction paper squares or rectangles in half.
   b. Sketch half of a flower outline on each with the center of flower on the fold.
   c. Cut along the outline; open to show the full flower.
4. Scatter the flowers over the bulletin board.

Other Ideas

1. Use a burlap background and cut flowers from felt.
2. Cover bulletin board with wallpaper.
3. Cut flowers from decorative paper such as foil or wrapping paper.
4. Use the board to keep track of memory work by placing a flower on the board each time a Bible verse is memorized.

CREATURES THAT CREEP AND CRAWL

Bible Story

God creates animal life. Genesis 1:24-25

Materials

White paper
Scissors
Stamp pads
Markers

Teacher Preparation

1. Cut paper to fit bulletin board.
2. Provide stamp pads and markers.

Classroom Activity

1. Stamp children's fingerprints over the paper, then wash hands with soap and warm water to remove ink from fingertips.
2. To create insects, use marker to add legs and feelers to the fingerprints.
3. Use fingerprints to outline the title "God's Creeping Creation" on the paper. Outline the letters and decorate with markers.
4. Attach the paper to the bulletin board. Talk about the ways God uses tiny insects to help in His world.

Other Ideas

1. Use fingerprints to form the bodies of animals.
2. Pour tempera paint on two folded paper towels placed on a paper plate. Use the paint instead of a stamp pad to create colorful fingerprints.
3. Stamp fingerprints from different-colored stamp pads.
4. Outline butterflies, then print fingerprint patterns on their wings.

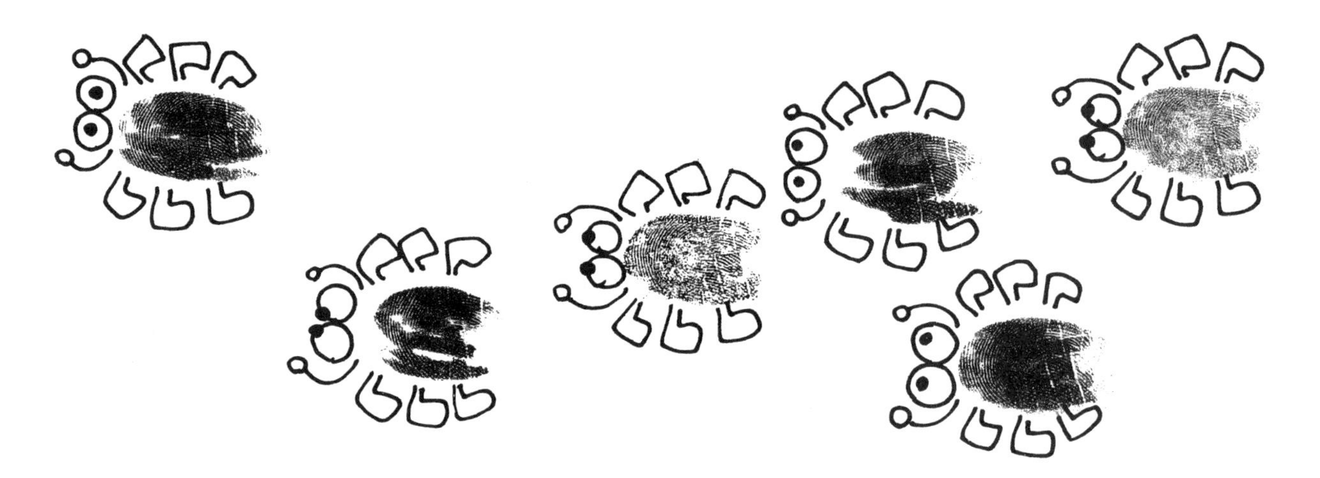

UNDER THE SEA

Bible Story

Creation of sea life. Genesis 1:20-23

Materials

Blue paper
Scissors
Drinking straws
Tempera paint (green and other colors)
Dish and spoon
Paper napkins
Paper plates
Raw potatoes
Knife
Paintbrushes
Markers

Teacher Preparation

1. Cut paper to fit bulletin board.
2. Cut several raw potatoes in half.
3. Pour green tempera paint in a dish. Put spoon beside it.
4. Put two folded paper napkins on a paper plate for each color you will use. Pour one color of paint on each paper plate for stamp pads.
5. Provide straws, paintbrushes, and markers.

Classroom Activity

1. Spoon green paint on the bottom of the blue paper. Using a drinking straw, blow paint upwards to make water plants. Let it dry thoroughly.
2. Talk about the many different kinds of sea life God made. Choose several to display on the bulletin board.
3. Dip potato halves into the paint and print on the paper, using as many different colors as you wish. Combine shapes to make coral or larger sea creatures.
4. Paint the title "God's Underwater World" on the paper.
5. When the paint is dry, draw fish details, such as eyes, fins, and tails, with markers. Attach the paper to the bulletin board.

Other Ideas

1. Draw fish with light crayons, then paint over them with a watercolor wash.
2. Omit straw blowing, and fingerpaint instead.

ALL CREATURES GREAT AND SMALL

Bible Story

Creation of land animals. Genesis 1:24-25

Materials

White paper
Construction paper
Glue
Scissors
Markers or crayons

Teacher Preparation

1. Cut white paper the size of bulletin board and attach to the board.
2. Provide construction paper, glue, scissors, and markers or crayons.
3. Cut construction paper letters for the title "All Creatures Great and Small." (Older children can cut out the letters themselves.)

Classroom Activity

1. Have each child choose an animal to make.
2. Draw the animal on construction paper and cut it out. Glue on pieces for ears, eyes, and other details. Curl, loop, and fold paper for a 3-D effect.
3. Add other details with markers or crayons.
4. Attach each animal to the bulletin board.
5. Glue letters for the title, "All Creatures Great and Small," to the board.
6. Let each child tell why he is glad God created the animal he added to the board.

Other Ideas

1. Draw a circle to represent the world. Attach the animals to it.
2. Draw animals directly on the white paper.
3. Paint green grass strokes on paper before attaching animals.

GOD'S SPECIAL CREATIONS

Bible Story

God creates people. Genesis 2:18-25

Materials

Colored paper
White paper plates
Markers or crayons
Construction paper
Yarn
Glue
Scissors

Teacher Preparation

1. Cut paper to fit bulletin board and attach to board.
2. Cut the title "God's Special Creations" from construction paper. (Older children can cut out the letters themselves.)
3. Provide paper plates, construction paper, yarn, glue, scissors, and markers or crayons.

Classroom Activity

1. Review the story of God's creation of Adam and Eve, our first grandparents. Discuss how Adam and Eve were unique creations by God, as we all are.
2. Attach the title, "God's Special Creations," to the bulletin board.
3. Make faces for Adam and Eve from two paper plates, using any combination of materials. Attach plates to the center of the bulletin board, and write their names under them.
4. Have children decorate paper plates to represent their faces. Attach them to the board. Print their names under the faces.

Other Ideas

1. Be creative in the materials you use to construct the faces.
2. Glue yarn for the title, "God's Special Creations," directly to the board.

TAKE CARE OF GOD'S WORLD

Bible Story

God tells Adam to take care of the garden. Genesis 2:15

Materials

Paper (gray and another color)
Trash
Brown paper bags
Crayons or markers
Glue
Stapler or thumbtacks
Plastic garbage bag
Scissors

Teacher Preparation

1. Cover the bulletin board with paper.
2. Draw and cut out the outline of a large trash can from a piece of gray paper. If needed, use an overhead projector to enlarge the pattern on page 17. (Older children can draw the trash can themselves.) Place the can at the center of the bulletin board.
3. Use thumbtacks to fasten the plastic trash bag to the bulletin board.
4. Provide brown paper bags, glue, and crayons or markers. Have stapler or thumbtacks accessible for use.

Classroom Activity

1. God asked Adam to take care of the new garden He had made. Talk about how God wants us to take care of His world today.
2. Have each child decorate a paper trash bag for picking up litter around your classroom and outside.
3. Attach pieces of litter to the top of the trash can, using a stapler or thumbtacks.
4. Place leftover trash in the plastic bag and encourage children to add additional litter as long as the bulletin board is up. Empty trash bag as needed.
5. Cut out letters for the title "Take Care of God's World" from colorful pieces of trash. Attach them to the bulletin board.

Other Ideas

1. Make a bulletin board illustrating an area before and after it has been cleared of litter.
2. Place additional brown paper bags and crayons on a table by the bulletin board. Encourage children to decorate the litter bags to take home and use.

TRASH CAN PATTERN

GOD'S FLOATING ZOO

Bible Story

The great flood. Genesis 6–9

Materials

Blue paper
Brown wrapping paper
Scissors
Markers or crayons
Construction paper
Glue

Teacher Preparation

1. Cut blue paper to fit bulletin board. Cover the board with it.
2. Draw the ark outline (page 19) on brown wrapping paper. If needed, use an overhead projector to enlarge the pattern. (Older children can draw the ark themselves.)
3. Provide construction paper, scissors, glue, and markers or crayons.

Classroom Activity

1. Divide the ark into rooms.
2. Draw animals on pieces of construction paper. Cut them out and glue them inside the ark. Draw Noah and his family and put them inside too.
3. God kept Noah, his family, and the animals safe from the rain and flood. Draw clouds, rain, and waves around the ark.
4. Use crayons or markers to write "God's Floating Zoo" on the blue paper.
5. God kept Noah and the animals safe from the flood. Talk about ways God keeps us safe today.

Other Ideas

1. Draw the ark, animals, water, and rain on a piece of white poster paper.
2. Glue animal crackers inside the ark to represent the animals.

SS3824

ARK PATTERN

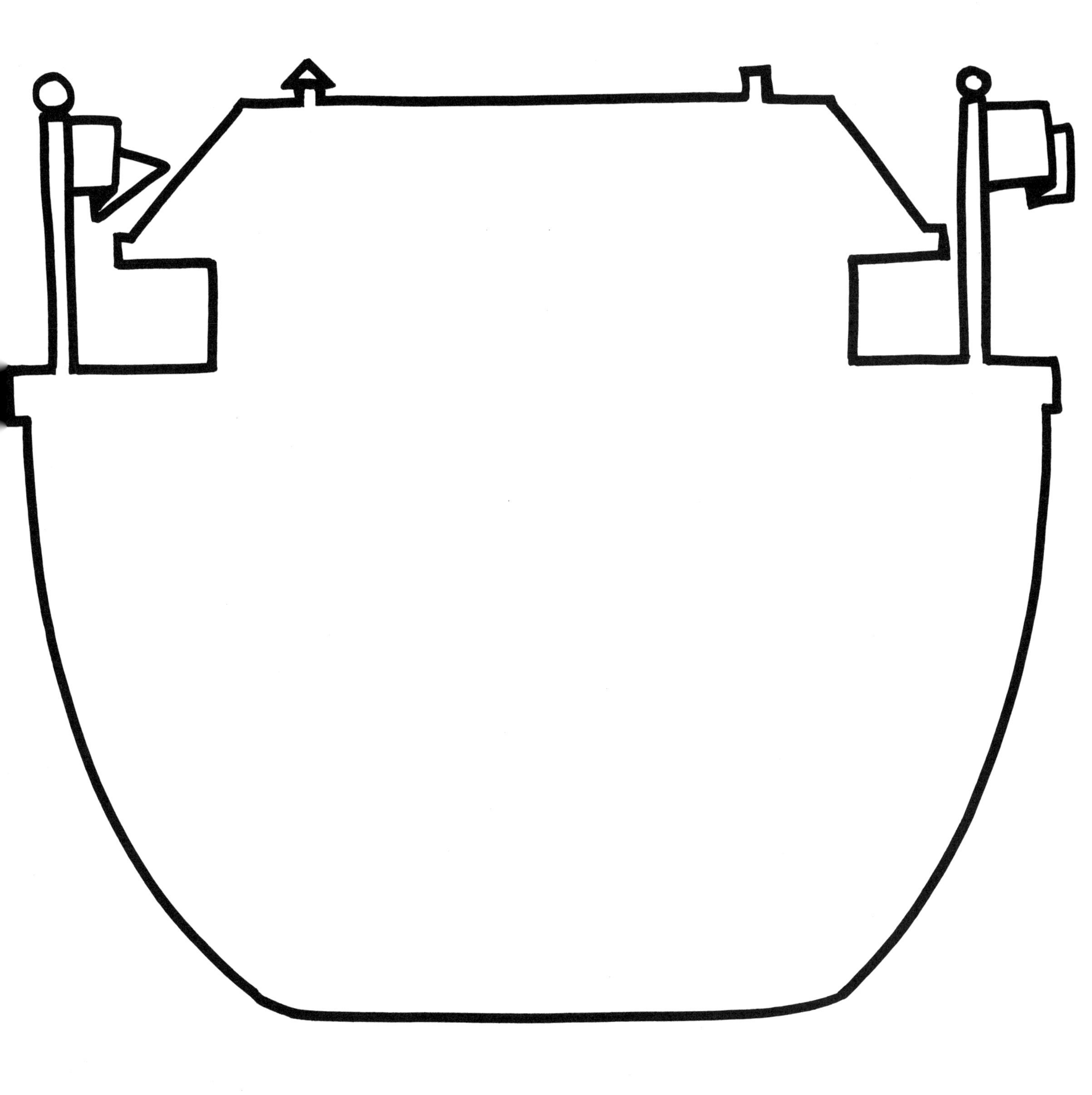

GOD KEEPS HIS PROMISES

bow in the sky. Genesis 9:12-17

Materials

Light blue paper
Construction paper in rainbow colors
Scissors
Glue
Cotton (optional)

Teacher Preparation

1. Cut blue paper to fit bulletin board.
2. Cut construction paper into strips.
3. Provide scissors, cotton (optional), and glue.
4. If needed, use an overhead projector to enlarge the rainbow pattern on page 21. Cut letters for title "God Keeps His Promises." (Older children can draw the rainbow and cut out the letters themselves.)

Classroom Activity

1. Cut colored strips into squares.
2. Glue the squares to the blue paper collage style to make a rainbow.
3. Glue letters for the title, "God Keeps His Promises," to the paper.
4. Attach the paper to the bulletin board.
5. The rainbow reminds us of the special promise God made that there would never be another great flood. What other promises did God make to His people? How did He keep His promises? What promises is God keeping today?

Other Ideas

1. Make the rainbow from fabric squares cut with pinking shears.
2. Under the rainbow, glue construction paper figures representing Bible people to whom God made and kept promises.
3. Draw or cut out the ark or Noah and his altar and attach them to the board under the rainbow.
4. Tear construction paper instead of cutting.

5. Make a rainbow from tissue paper cut into squares. Attach the squares with a mixture of white glue and water (one part each).
6. Twist tissue squares and glue them to the picture.
7. Outline the rainbow with yarn.

RAINBOW PATTERN

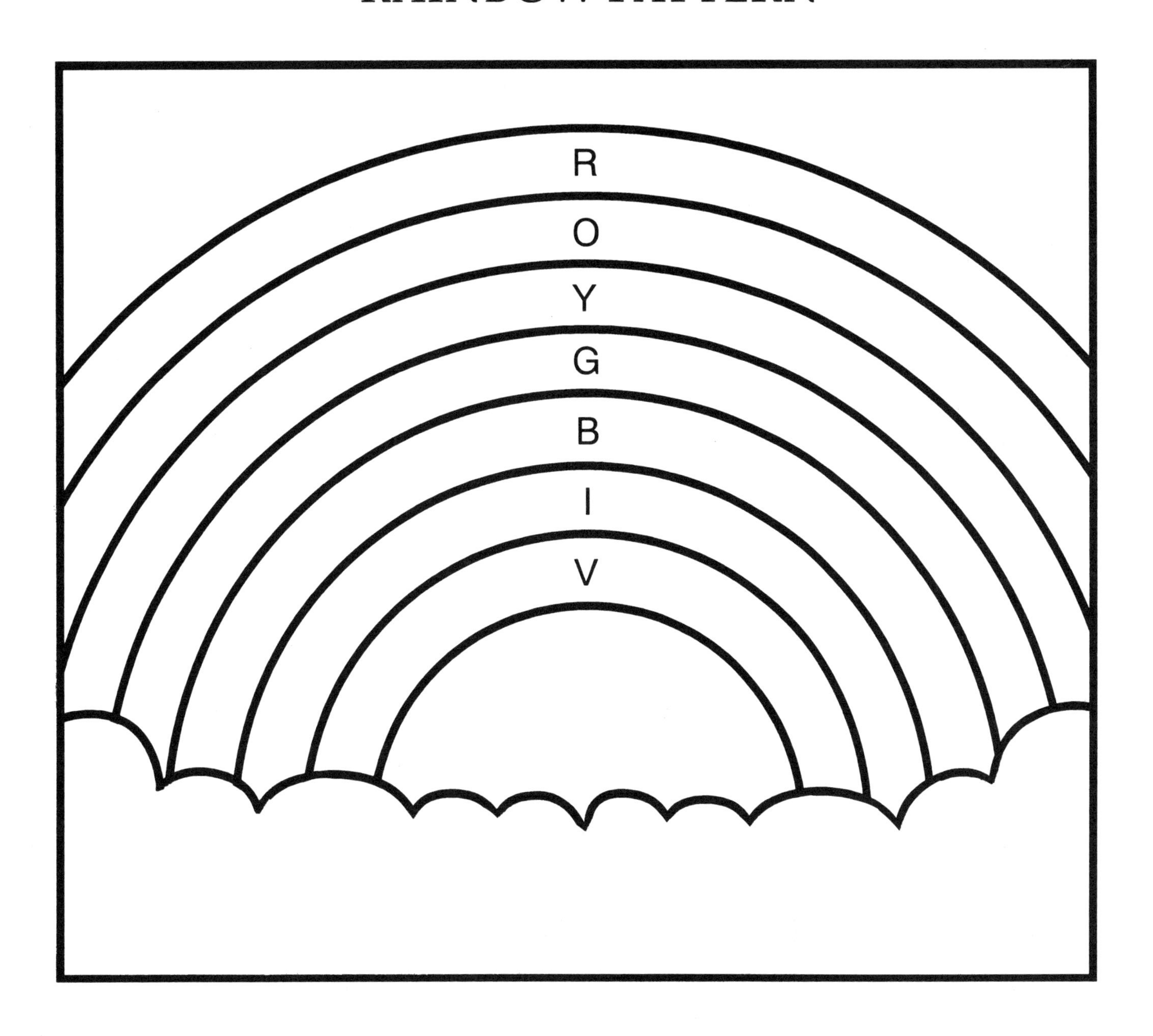

COLOR CODE

Red	Blue
Orange	Indigo
Yellow	Violet
Green	

GOD GOES WITH US

Bible Story

God calls Abraham to go to a new land. Genesis 12:1-9

Materials

Paper
Scissors
Toy cars
Tempera paint
Paper towels
Paper plate
Paintbrush
Detergent (optional)

Teacher Preparation

1. Cut paper to fit the bulletin board.
2. Gather several toy cars, preferably those with textured wheels.
3. Fold paper towels. Place them on the paper plate and add tempera paint. (A few drops of detergent added to the tempera will aid in cleanup.)

Classroom Activity

1. Talk about how Abraham might travel today. Compare the way God went with Abraham long ago and the way God goes with us today.
2. Take turns rolling the wheels of toy cars in tempera, then running them over the paper to make tire tracks. Wash wheels in warm, soapy water.
3. Paint the title "God Goes with Us" at the top of the paper.
4. Attach the paper to the bulletin board.

Other Ideas

1. Print tire tracks on a map background.
2. Print several different colors of tire tracks.
3. Encourage each child to write "God goes with (child's name) when (he/she) goes to (fill in place name)" along the track he has made.
4. Use this activity with other stories telling of God's care for His people during their travels.

COUNT THE STARS

Bible Story

God's promise to Abraham. Genesis 15:5-6

Materials

Dark blue paper
Scissors
Gummed stars
Aluminum foil
Glue

Teacher Preparation

1. Cut paper to fit the bulletin board. Attach it to the board.
2. Cut foil letters for title "Count the Stars if You Can." (Older children can cut out letters for the title.)
3. Provide gummed stars, aluminum foil, scissors, and glue.

Classroom Activity

1. Attach letters for the title, "Count the Stars if You Can," on the bulletin board.
2. Stick gummed stars on the blue paper.
3. Cut an aluminum foil star larger than the others and attach it to the board. (To make a star pattern, fold a square in half, trace half the star on the square, cut it out, and unfold it.)
4. Read God's promise to Abraham in the Bible. Point out that one of the children that came from Abraham's family was Jesus. Find the big star that reminds us of Him.

Other Ideas

1. Draw stars and letters on white paper, using light-colored crayons, then cover the paper with a dark, watercolor wash.
2. Cut stars from different colors of art foil or from aluminum foil.
3. Cut stars from different colors of construction paper.
4. Add a silhouette of Abraham to the bottom of the bulletin board.

A GIFT OF LAUGHTER

Bible Story

Isaac is born. Genesis 21:1-17

Materials

White paper
Paper plates (2 large, 1 small)
Newspaper
Scissors
Glue
Markers
Wallpaper

Teacher Preparation

1. Attach the paper to the bulletin board.
2. Cut newspaper into long strips. Cut letters for the title "God Brought Them Laughter" from wallpaper. (Older children can cut out their own strips and letters.)
3. Provide newspaper, wallpaper, scissors, glue, paper plates, and markers.

Classroom Activity

1. Abraham and Sarah had waited many years for the birth of their son. How do you think they felt when Isaac was born? Do you think they laughed? The name Isaac means "laughter." What are some ways you bring happiness to your home?
2. Decide which class members will do the following tasks for the completion of the bulletin board:
   a. Cut newspaper into strips for hair and beard. Curl strips over the edge of scissors.
   b. Draw faces for Abraham and Sarah on the large paper plates.
   c. Draw a face for Isaac on the small paper plate.
   d. Cut a wallpaper body for each face.
   e. Use markers to draw hands, feet, and other details.
   f. Cut wallpaper or newspaper letters for the title, "God Brought Them Laughter."
3. Attach the lettering and paper plate faces to the bulletin board. Add the wallpaper bodies. Glue on newspaper strips for hair and beard.

Other Ideas

1. Draw the three figures directly on the poster paper.
2. Use yarn instead of newspaper for hair and beard.

PART OF GOD'S FAMILY

Bible Story

The birth of Isaac. Genesis 21:1-7

Materials

Light-colored paper
Wallpaper
White drawing paper
Scissors
Markers
Glue

Teacher Preparation

1. Attach paper to the bulletin board.
2. Cut wallpaper letters for the title "Part of God's Family." (Older children can cut out the letters themselves.)
3. Provide wallpaper, scissors, markers, white drawing paper, and glue.

Classroom Activity

1. How many people did Isaac have in his family? How many do you have? Make a house and draw your family in it to put on the bulletin board. Let it remind you to thank God for His gift of families.
2. Cut wallpaper into a house shape. Cut a door as shown in the diagram. Fold out the door as indicated.
3. Cut a piece of white drawing paper and glue it behind the open door.
4. Have each child draw his family inside the open door. Draw windows and decorative features on each house. Attach the houses to the bulletin board.
5. Glue wallpaper letters for the title, "Part of God's Family," on the board. This board reminds us that we are all part of God's family.

Other Ideas

1. Cut houses from construction paper.
2. Cut one big house with windows that open to show different children in the class. This may be especially appropriate if children in your class come from dysfunctional families. For them it may be better to stress the ultimate love and security found in the family of God instead of their earthly homes.

TOOLS FOR GOD'S HELPERS

Bible Story

Rebekah and Abraham's servant.
Genesis 24

Materials

White paper
Construction paper
Scissors
Pencils
Different kinds of tools
Glue

Teacher Preparation

1. Attach white paper to the bulletin board.
2. Gather kitchen or workroom tools that are safe for children to trace around.
3. Draw and cut out a large water jar, using the pattern on page 27. If needed, use an overhead projector to enlarge the pattern. (Older children can draw the water jar themselves.) Attach the water jar to the center of the board.
4. Cut letters for the title "Tools for God's Helpers" from construction paper. (Older children can cut the letters themselves.)
5. Provide construction paper, pencils, scissors, and glue.

Classroom Activity

1. Talk about how Rebekah used her water jar to help Abraham's servant. Talk about the tools that have been brought into the classroom. Tell how each one is used to help people. How can these tools be used to help the Lord? (Emphasize that we help the Lord when we help others.)
2. Glue the title, "Tools for God's Helpers," on the water jar.
3. Outline the tools on construction paper and cut them out.
4. Glue the tools to the bulletin board.

Other Ideas

1. Cut the tools from newspaper or corrugated cardboard.
2. Trace the tools directly on the paper.
3. Make a smaller water jar and glue the letters directly to the paper.

WATER JAR PATTERN

BIBLE COUPLES

Bible Story

Rebekah and Isaac. Genesis 24:61-67

Materials

Wallpaper
White drawing paper
Construction paper
Colored pencils
Scissors
Glue

Teacher Preparation

1. Cover bulletin board with wallpaper.
2. Cut rectangle from white drawing paper; cut construction paper rectangles about 2" longer and wider.
3. Cut the title "Bible Couples" from construction paper. (Older children can cut the letters themselves.)
4. Provide colored pencils and glue.

Classroom Activity

1. Rebekah and Isaac are only one of many Bible couples. Look through your Bible to find the names of more couples. Write the names of some of these couples on the board and tell something about each.
2. Let each child pick a couple from the list to draw a picture of on the white drawing paper, using colored pencils. The drawings may look like the couple's wedding pictures.
3. Glue the completed drawings to construction paper.
4. Write the name of each couple at the bottom of each picture.
5. Glue the title, "Bible Couples," to the bulletin board.
6. Attach the pictures to the wallpaper background.

Other Ideas

1. Glue swirls of yarn around the paper frames.
2. Use a plain background for the boards, and cut the frames from wallpaper.
3. Cut the sides of each picture like the edges of a photograph.
4. Glue the pictures inside Styrofoam™ trays.

GOD IS NEAR

Bible Story

Jacob's dream. Genesis 28:10-22

Materials

Blue burlap
White and yellow yarn
Scissors
White glue
Fabric scraps
Colored glue
Pencils

Teacher Preparation

1. Cut burlap to fit the bulletin board.
2. Provide fabric scraps, yarn, scissors, pencils, and white and colored glue.

Classroom Activity

1. In Jacob's dream, angels walked up and down a stairway to heaven with God standing at the very top, assuring Jacob of His constant love and presence. Talk about God's presence in each child's life.
2. Glue a yellow yarn stairway to the burlap.
3. Draw and cut angels from fabric and glue them on the stairway.
4. Cut sleeping Jacob from fabric and glue him beneath the stairway.
5. Use colored glue to add details to the angels and to Jacob. Write the title "God Is Near" on the burlap, using colored glue. Let it dry.
6. Attach the burlap to the bulletin board.

Other Ideas

1. Cut letters from fabric scraps.
2. Cut fabric with pinking shears.
3. Outline fabric with colored glue.
4. Glue yarn to colored paper.
5. Use light-colored crayons to draw the picture and title on a sheet of white paper, then brush over them with a watercolor wash.

JOSEPH'S COLORFUL LIFE

Bible Story

Joseph's coat of many colors. Genesis 37:3

Materials

White paper
Colored tissue paper
Water in a dish
Sponge
Markers
Pencil
Construction paper
Scissors

Teacher Preparation

1. Cut white paper to fit the bulletin board.
2. Draw a pencil outline of Joseph and the title "Joseph's Colorful Life" on the paper. Use an overhead projector to enlarge the pattern on page 31. (Older children can draw the picture and the lettering themselves.)
3. Cut circles from different colors of construction paper. Cut a circle for each story in Joseph's life that you are studying.
4. Provide tissue paper, scissors, water, sponge, and markers.

Classroom Activity

1. Cut bright-colored tissue paper into long strips for Joseph's coat. Cut small squares for the lettering. Cut small brown or black strips for Joseph's hair.
2. Sponge water over Joseph's hair and coat.
3. Lay long strips of tissue paper over Joseph's coat. Do not put complimentary colors (red/green, blue/orange, yellow/purple) together. Trim strips as needed at the edge of the coat. Fill letters with colored squares and Joseph's hair with brown strips. Sponge with water one more time.
4. Pull off the tissue after several minutes. For more intense color, let the tissue dry before removing it.
5. When dry, use markers to outline Joseph and the letters in title.
6. Attach the paper to the bulletin board.
7. As you study different stories about Joseph's life, draw pictures to illustrate them inside the construction paper circles. Place the circles around Joseph on the bulletin board.

Other Ideas

1. Tear tissue paper instead of cutting it.
2. Glue tissue paper on with a mixture of glue and water (one part each).
3. Use crepe paper for brighter colors.
4. Glue pieces of fabric or construction paper over the coat and letters in title.
5. Cover Joseph with different colors of yarn.
6. Use a solid color for the background and cut Joseph from a separate sheet of white paper.
7. Drop water (mixed with food coloring) from eyedroppers onto paper towels. When dry, glue over Joseph's coat.

JOSEPH PATTERN

FORGIVE ONE ANOTHER

Bible Story

Joseph forgives his brothers.
Genesis 45

Materials

White paper
Red construction paper
Cardboard
Scissors
Peeled crayons (red, pink, and purple)

Teacher Preparation

1. Cut white paper to fit the bulletin board.
2. Cut cardboard hearts in different sizes. To cut a heart pattern, fold a piece of paper in half and cut out half a heart, then unfold. (Older children can cut out hearts themselves.)
3. Cut a large construction paper heart and write the title "Forgive One Another" on it. (Older children can do this themselves.) Glue the heart to the center of the white paper.
4. Provide crayons from which you have removed the paper.

Classroom Activity

1. What do you think Joseph's brothers expected when they found out what had happened to the brother they had sold into slavery? Why did Joseph forgive them? Ask God to help you forgive others as Joseph did.
2. Place each cardboard heart under the white paper and rub over it with a peeled crayon. Fill the paper around the center heart with heart rubbings of different sizes and colors.
3. Attach the paper to the bulletin board.
4. The hearts remind us that Jesus wants us to forgive others.

Other Ideas

1. Create a concentric pattern of hearts with blank space around the center heart.
2. Cut the center and surrounding hearts from construction paper.
3. Cut heart shapes from sponges. Dip them in paint and stamp hearts on the paper.

CHILDREN OF THE PROMISE

Bible Story

Jacob blesses his sons.
Genesis 49:1-28

Materials

Light-colored paper
Scissors
Markers
Thumbtacks
Glue
12 Styrofoam™ cups
Construction paper

Teacher Preparation

1. Cut paper to fit the bulletin board. Attach it to the board.
2. Cut out construction paper letters for the title "Children of the Promise." (Older children can cut out letters themselves.)
3. Provide Styrofoam™ cups, construction paper, scissors, glue, markers, and thumbtacks.

Classroom Activity

1. Review the names and significance of each of Jacob's twelve sons. Talk about how God was keeping His promise to Abraham through them.
2. Divide the sons among the class. Make a cup puppet for each son.
3. Cut eyes, nose, mouth, and hair from construction paper and glue to the cup puppets.
4. When finished, tack each puppet to the bulletin board and write the puppet's name under each one.
5. Glue the title, "Children of the Promise," to the bulletin board.

Other Ideas

1. Use permanent markers to draw features on Styrofoam™ cups.
2. Make faces on strips of paper and roll them into tube puppets, or cover oatmeal boxes with construction paper and decorate each one with a face.
3. Glue yarn hair to the puppets.

IN HIS HANDS

Bible Story

The birth of Moses. Exodus 2:1-10

Materials

Light blue burlap
Yarn in assorted colors
Scissors
Glue
Chalk
Ruler

Teacher Preparation

1. Cut burlap to fit the bulletin board.
2. Enlarge the pattern of Moses in the basket and the lettering (page 35). Trace it on burlap with chalk. Use an overhead projector to enlarge the pattern. (Older children can draw the pattern and lettering themselves.)
3. Cut yarn into 24" lengths.
4. Provide scissors and glue.

Classroom Activity

1. Sing the song "He's Got the Whole World in His Hands" substituting the words: "He had Moses in the basket in His hands" for the first three lines of the verse. Talk about how it makes you feel to know that God watches over you as He once watched over baby Moses.
2. Pick colors of yarn needed for the picture and lettering; decide who will glue them on.
3. Cut yarn into sizes needed for gluing. (Cut yarn ahead of time for young children.)
4. Take turns gluing yarn on the burlap picture.
5. When the glue is dry, attach the burlap to the bulletin board.

Other Ideas

1. Sew yarn on burlap with dull tapestry needles.
2. Glue felt scraps on the burlap.
3. Draw on burlap with colored glue.

MOSES PATTERN

IN HIS HANDS

I HAVE CALLED YOU

Bible Story

Moses sees a burning bush.
Exodus 3:1–4:17

Materials

White paper
Red, yellow, and orange tissue paper
Brown yarn
Scissors
White glue and water (1 part each)
Cup
Sponge brush
Ruler

Teacher Preparation

1. Cut white paper to fit the bulletin board.
2. Cut large sheets of tissue paper into small ones for easier use by the children. Cut yarn into 24" lengths.
3. Mix white glue and water in a cup.
4. Provide scissors and sponge brush.

Classroom Activity

1. Tear tissue paper into different-sized pieces.
2. Brush the mixture of water and glue over the paper, then add tissue paper pieces. Brush again with the water and glue mixture.
3. Cut brown yarn and glue over the tissue pieces to make a trunk and branches.
4. Glue yarn for the title "I Have Called You." God called Moses through the burning bush to do a special job for Him. Talk about the special job God has for each of us to do.
5. Attach the paper to the bulletin board.

Other Ideas

1. Use a dull tapestry needle to stitch the outline of the bush's branches on paper or burlap.
2. Paint the bush's branches; sponge paint the flames.
3. Cut letters from tissue paper; use rubber cement to attach them to the paper.
4. Add names of children in the class to the bulletin board.

THE LORD IS MY STRENGTH

Bible Story

Moses' song. Exodus 15:1-18

Materials

White paper
Blue finger paint
Cookie sheet
Markers
Newspapers
Scissors

Teacher Preparation

1. Cut paper to fit the bulletin board. Lay it on newspapers on a table.
2. Pour blue finger paint on the cookie sheet.
3. Provide markers.

Classroom Activity

1. Take turns finger painting waves on the white paper. Try to swirl paint upwards on each side toward the middle to create parting waves.
2. When dry, use markers to write these words down the space in the middle of the water: "The Lord is my strength and my song; he has become my salvation." Exodus 15:2a
3. Attach the paper to the bulletin board. Read "The Song of Moses" from which these words were taken. Talk about how God is our "strength and salvation."

Other Ideas

1. Draw the children of Israel crossing through the Red Sea in the center of board.
2. Write more words from "The Song of Moses" on the bulletin board.

SING TO THE LORD

Bible Story

Miriam's song of praise. Exodus 15:19-21

Materials

White paper
Colored tape (plastic or masking)
Yarn
Construction paper
Markers or crayons
Glue
Children's hymnbooks
Scissors

Teacher Preparation

1. Cut white paper to fit the bulletin board.
2. Use tape to mark off the five lines of the music staff on the paper.
3. Use yarn to outline a treble clef on the staff.
4. Write the title "Sing to the Lord" along the top of the paper. (Older children can write the title themselves.)
5. Attach the paper to the bulletin board.
6. Cut a construction paper circle for each child.
7. Provide glue, hymnbooks, and markers or crayons.

Classroom Activity

1. Read the story of Miriam's song of praise from the Bible. What song would you have sung if you had been Miriam?
2. Have each child write the words to a favorite gospel song in a circle. Encourage students to check hymnbooks for correct wording, or simply write the words as they remember them.
3. Glue the circles to the staff to be notes. Use tape or yarn to make stems for the notes.
4. Sing the songs written on the notes.

Other Ideas

1. Add a second staff with a bass clef to the bulletin board.
2. Write just the title of a favorite Christian song in each note.
3. Place the notes to make the tune of a favorite song.

BREAD FROM THE LORD

Bible Story

Manna in the wilderness. Exodus 16

Materials

Light-colored paper
Markers
Wrappers and packaging from bread products
Tacks and stapler

Teacher Preparation

1. Attach paper to the bulletin board.
2. Gather together old bread wrappers and other commercial packaging from bread products. (You may want to send a note home the week before you make the bulletin board, asking parents to save bread wrappers.)

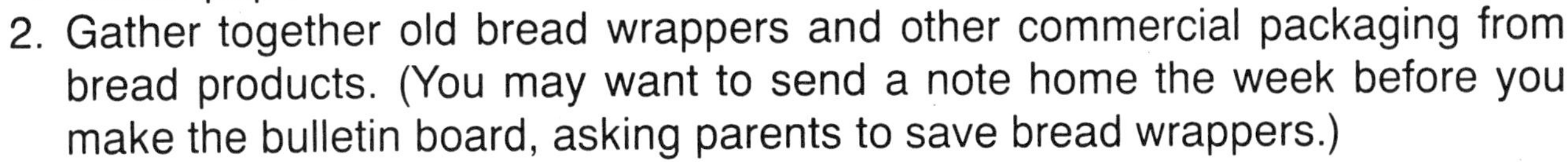

3. Write the title “Bread from the Lord” on the board. (Older children can write the titles themselves.)
4. Provide tacks and a stapler.

Classroom Activity

1. Talk about how God, who gave manna to the children of Israel in the wilderness, also gives bread to us today.
2. Staple bread wrappers and packages to the bulletin board. Use tacks for heavier pieces.

Other Ideas

1. Draw a basket on the bulletin board and glue items as if they are in the basket.
2. Make two drawings on the bulletin board, one showing the Israelites with manna, the other showing children today with bread products.
3. Cut letters for the title, “Bread from the Lord,” from bread packages. Outline with black marker.

GOD'S GOOD COMMANDMENTS

Bible Story

The Ten Commandments. Exodus 20:1-17

Materials

Colored paper
White poster board
Magazines and newspapers
Glue
Scissors
Stapler
Acetate (optional)

Teacher Preparation

1. Attach colored paper to the bulletin board.
2. Cut white poster board into two connecting tablets. Enlarge the pattern on page 41. (Older children can cut out the tablets themselves.)
3. Provide magazines, newspapers, scissors, glue, and stapler.

Classroom Activity

1. Read the Ten Commandments in Exodus 20. Talk about what the home, school, and community would be like to live in if all people followed God's Commandments.
2. Divide the Commandments among the class.
3. Look through magazines and newspapers to find letters for the words of each commandment. Cut them out.
4. Cut out large letters for the title "God's Good Commandments." Glue them to the top of the board.
5. Take turns gluing letters for individual commandments in order on the poster board tablets. You may want to glue each commandment on a sheet of paper before gluing it to the tablet.
6. Staple the tablets to the board.

Other Ideas

1. Use markers to write the Commandments directly on the tablets.
2. Draw an illustration for each commandment and add it to the board.

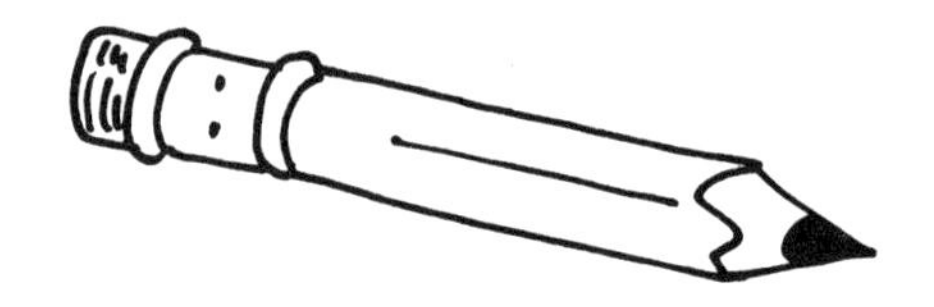

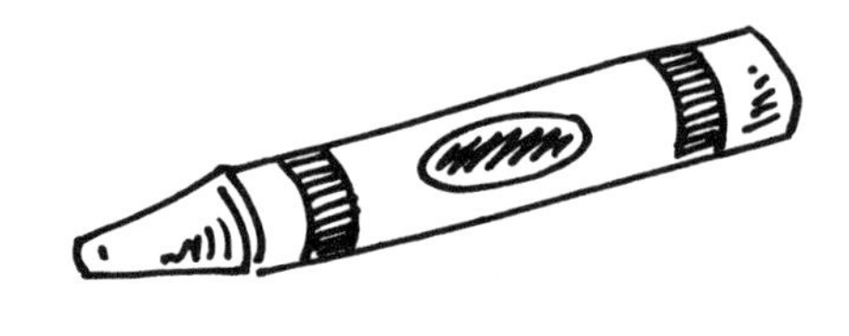

TEN COMMANDMENTS PATTERN

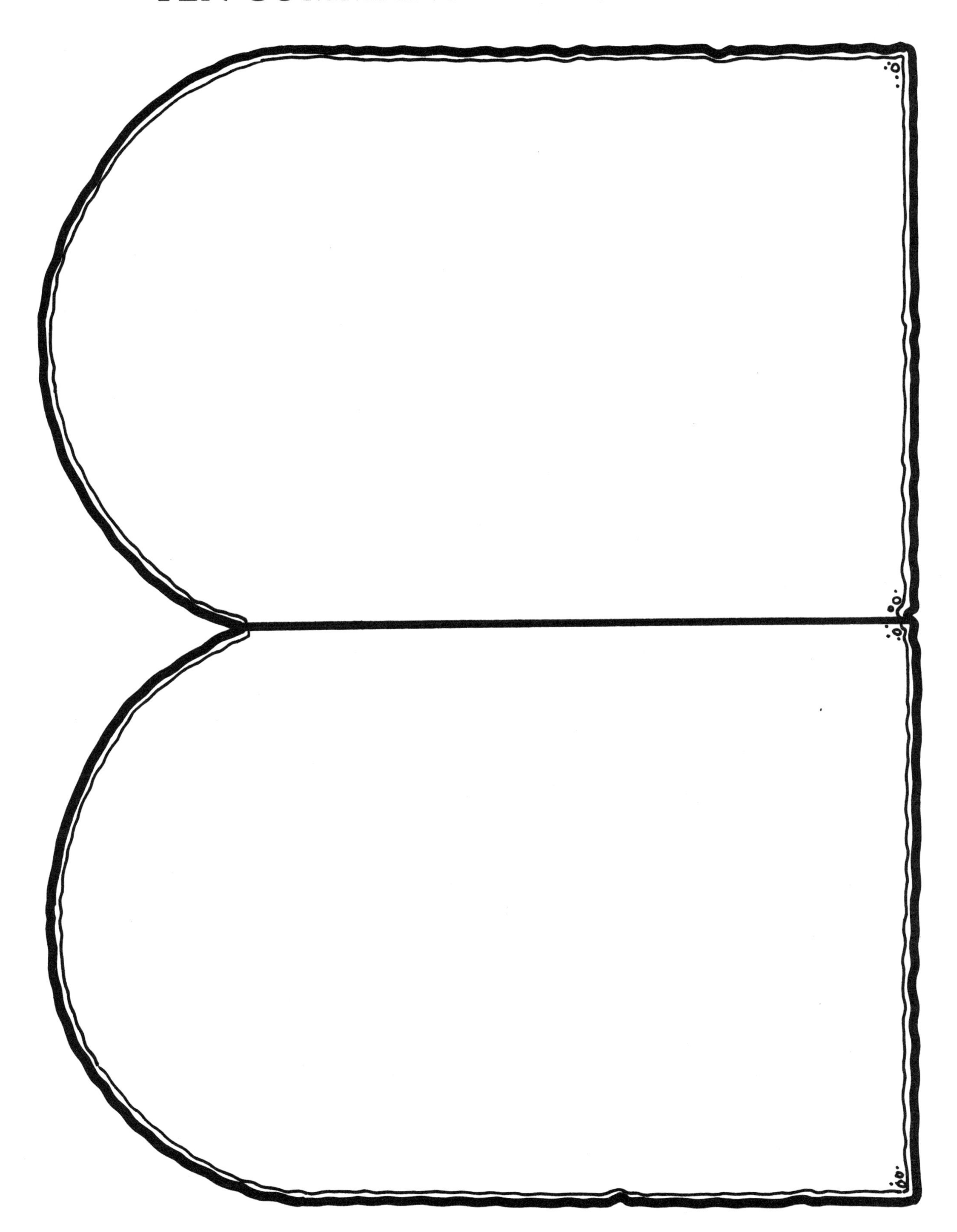

THE LORD IS MY SHEPHERD

Bible Story

The Lord is my Shepherd. Psalm 23

Materials

Green fabric (with small flower print)
Felt (white, pink, tan, and black)
Cotton balls
Fabric scraps
White glue
Colored glue
Scissors

Teacher Preparation

1. Cut green fabric to fit the bulletin board.
2. From white felt, cut circles for the sheep bodies and ovals for their heads; cut narrow black rectangles for legs.
3. Cut a pink or tan felt circle for David's head, and a fabric triangle for his body. (Older children can cut out felt pieces themselves.)
4. Provide cotton, fabric scraps, scissors, white glue, and colored glue.

Classroom Activity

1. Glue shapes together to make sheep; then glue them to the green fabric.
2. Glue David's head to the fabric triangle, then glue them both to the green fabric. Cut felt or fabric to make hair, feet, or other details, including a staff for David to hold.
3. Use colored glue to add other details.
4. Glue cotton balls to the sheep.
5. Use colored glue to write the title "The Lord Is My Shepherd" on the banner. Talk about ways David took care of his sheep that remind us of how God takes care of us.
6. Attach the green fabric to the bulletin board.

Other Ideas

1. Outline fabric with colored glue.
2. Cut construction paper shapes to glue to a paper background.
3. Make the bulletin board from different kinds of wrapping paper.

PRAISE THE LORD

Bible Story

David plays for Saul.
1 Samuel 16:14-23

Materials

White paper
Scissors
Tempera paint in bright colors
Large paintbrushes
Water in a container
Newspapers
Tapes of Christian songs
Markers

Teacher Preparation

1. Cut white paper to fit the bulletin board. Place on newspaper covered work area.
2. Get tapes of Christian songs ready to play.
3. Provide markers, paint, container of water, and brushes.

Classroom Activity

1. Take turns painting tempera paint on the white paper, using large arm motions. Listen to Christian songs as you work.
2. When the paint is dry, use dark markers to write "Praise the Lord" in large letters on the painting. (The teacher can do this for young children.)
3. Read some of the songs of praise David wrote in the book of Psalms. Let each child pick words from a Psalm to write on the paper.
4. Attach the paper to the bulletin board.

Other Ideas

1. Draw on the paper with crayons, markers, or colored glue.
2. Cut out the letters for the title, "Praise the Lord," from paper decorated by painting. Glue the letters to a plain piece of paper.
3. Write "Praise the Lord" on the board in large letters. Fill the letters with colorful pieces of construction, wrapping, or tissue paper.
4. Make up words of praise as David did, and write them on the paper.

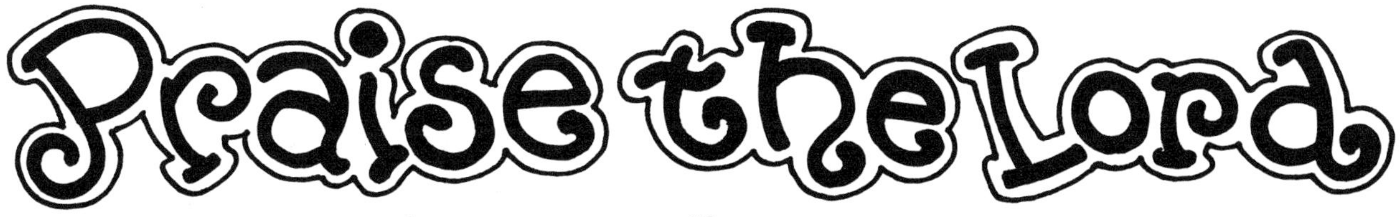

THE HOUSE OF THE LORD

Bible Story

Solomon builds the temple. 1 Kings 6

Materials

Light-colored paper
Box lids
Construction paper
Scissors
Glue
Tacks or stapler

Teacher Preparation

1. Attach light-colored paper to the bulletin board.
2. The week before you plan to do this bulletin board, send a note home with each student, asking parents to save cardboard box lids for class use.
3. Cut construction paper letters for the title "The House of the Lord." (Older children can cut out the letters themselves.)
4. Provide glue, construction paper, box lids, and scissors. Have tacks or a stapler available.

Classroom Activity

1. Imagine what it might have been like to see Solomon's temple being built. Read the biblical account of its building.
2. Let each child pick out a box lid to decorate and add to the bulletin board. Options for decorating lids are:
   a. Cut a construction paper strip, accordion fold it, and glue each end to opposite sides of the lid.
   b. Cut construction paper to fit and glue inside a box lid.
   c. Cut some other construction paper pattern to put inside the lid.
3. Glue letters for the title, "The House of the Lord," to the top of the board.
4. Tack or staple the lids together on the board to make a temple outline.

Other Ideas

1. Make the temple outline from small, painted boxes.
2. Put together different kinds of flat corrugated cardboard to create the temple.

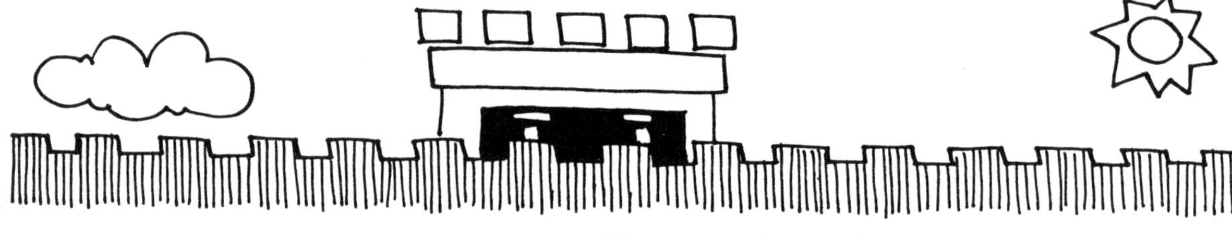

COME AND WORSHIP

Bible Story

Solomon dedicates the temple.
1 Kings 8:62-66

Materials

White paper
Markers or crayons
Scissors

Teacher Preparation

1. Cut white paper to fit the bulletin board.
2. Check a Bible dictionary or handbook to find out what worship was like at the time of King Solomon.

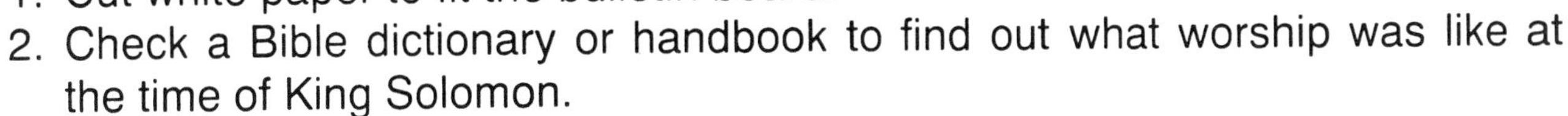

3. Provide markers or crayons.

Classroom Activity

1. Compare worship during Solomon's time and worship today. Ask children to share how their churches worship.
2. Draw the inside of a church from the top, side, or front with a worship service taking place.
3. Write "Come and Worship at (*name of your church*)" on the top of the sheet.
4. Attach the completed picture to the bulletin board.

Other Ideas

1. Cut the outline of the church from a large sheet of paper.
2. Cut the parts of the church from different colors of construction paper. Add foil or textured material.
3. Paint the worship scene with tempera paint.
4. Write the times of services at your church on the board.
5. Have each child add a picture of herself worshiping in church.

GOD HEARD JONAH'S PRAYER

Bible Story

Jonah and the fish. Jonah 1–2

Materials

Blue and green paper
Newspapers
Stapler
Markers
Scissors

Teacher Preparation

1. Attach blue paper to the bulletin board.
2. Cut large fish shapes from green paper. Enlarge the fish pattern on page 47.
3. Write the title "God Heard Jonah's Prayer" on the blue paper. (Older children can cut out the fish and write letters for the title themselves.)
4. Provide markers, scissors, and newspapers, and have a stapler available.

Classroom Activity

1. Decide who will do each of the following activities needed to finish the bulletin board.
   a. Draw wave lines over the blue paper.
   b. Draw Jonah and draw scales, fins, an eye, and other features on the fish.
   c. After the teacher staples partly around the fish shape, wad and stick newspaper under the fish to "puff" it out. When it's stuffed, have the teacher finish stapling.
   d. Cut and decorate other smaller fish to stuff and attach to the board.
   e. Add construction paper sea plants and other underwater creatures.
2. Have students share times they have prayed to God in time of need and, like Jonah, were heard.

Other Ideas

1. Cut the fish from white paper. Color it with crayon rubbings.
2. Staple two pieces of paper together to make the fish and stuff it. Then hang it by thread or yarn from the top of the bulletin board.
3. Glue the fish, without the stuffing, to the bulletin board.
4. Make the fish from construction paper.
5. Don't staple the mouth of the fish. Stuff a figure to represent Jonah, and attach it to the inside of the stuffed fish's mouth with a string. Take turns putting Jonah in and out as you tell the story.

FISH PATTERN

GOD GIVES US FOOD

Bible Story

Elijah is fed by ravens. 1 Kings 17:1-6

Materials

Paper tablecloth (with pattern, if possible)
Paper plates
Glue
Construction paper
Scissors
Thumbtacks
Markers or crayons

Teacher Preparation

1. Attach paper tablecloth to the bulletin board.
2. Cut letters for the title "Our Food Comes from the Lord" from dark construction paper and glue them to the center of the tablecloth. (Older children can cut out the letters for the title themselves.)
3. Provide paper plates, construction paper, glue, markers or crayons, and scissors.

Classroom Activity

1. Review the story of the ravens bringing food to Elijah. Discuss how God gives us food today.
2. Have children draw food shapes on construction paper and cut them out. Glue them to paper plates.
3. Thumbtack the plates to the board around the title.

Other Ideas

1. Add napkins, paper cups, and plastic tableware next to the plates.
2. Draw a tablecloth pattern on white paper for the background.
3. Use markers or crayons to draw food on the paper plates.
4. Use this board with other lessons emphasizing God's gift of food for us.
5. Use a plastic tablecloth instead of a paper one.

THE LORD IS GOD

Bible Story

Elijah and the prophets of Baal.
1 Kings 18:20-40

Materials

White paper
2 sponges
Scissors
Gray and red tempera paint
2 paper plates
4 paper towels
Pencil with an eraser
Newspaper

Teacher Preparation

1. Cut white paper to fit the bulletin board.

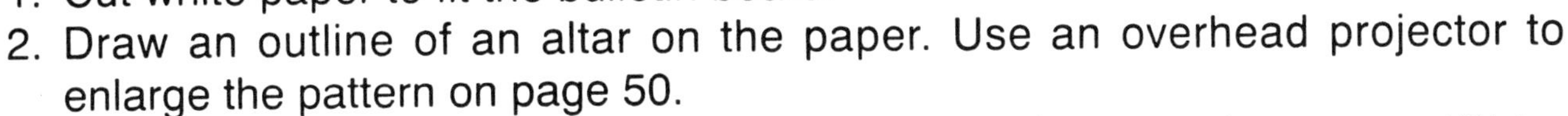

2. Draw an outline of an altar on the paper. Use an overhead projector to enlarge the pattern on page 50.
3. Draw outline letters for the title "The Lord Is God" on the paper. (Older children can draw the outline for the altar and the title themselves.)
4. Cut one sponge into a rock-shaped oval; cut the other into the shape of a flame.
5. Place two paper towels on each paper plate. Pour one of the tempera colors on each plate to make stamp pads.
6. Provide pencil eraser.

Classroom Activity

1. Take turns stamping stone shapes on the altar and flame shapes on top of it.
2. Use the pencil eraser to stamp inside the letters at the top of the paper.
3. Attach the paper to the bulletin board.
4. Talk about how brave Elijah was to stand up to those who did not believe in God. Discuss times in our lives when we need God's help to stand up for our beliefs.

Other Ideas

1. Cut flames and stones from construction paper or wallpaper.
2. Paint the title "The Lord Is God."

ALTAR PATTERN

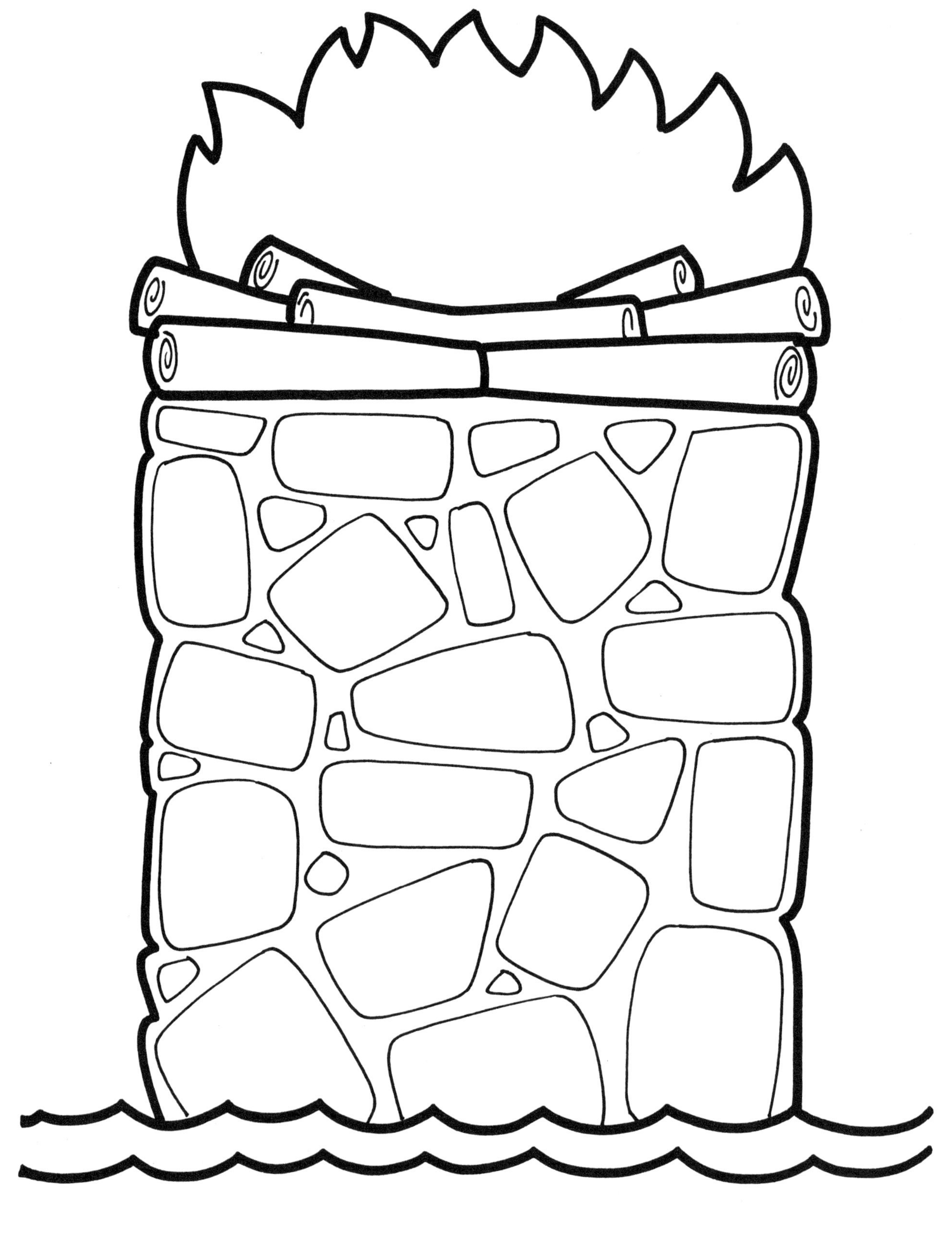

OUR GOD CAN SAVE US

Bible Story

Three men in the fiery furnace. Daniel 3

Materials

White paper
Crepe paper (red, yellow, and orange)
Sponge
Water in a dish
Markers
Chenille stems
Scissors
Glue or stapler

Teacher Preparation

1. Cut white paper to fit the bulletin board.
2. Cut crepe paper into strips easily handled by children.
3. Provide water in a dish, sponge, markers, chenille stems, and crepe paper.

Classroom Activity

1. Let everyone take a strip of crepe paper to tear into small pieces.
2. Sponge water over the white paper, and stick on the torn crepe paper. Then sponge water over the paper. Remove the crepe paper after several minutes or when dry.
3. Write the title "Our God Can Save Us" on the white paper.
4. Attach the paper to the bulletin board.
5. Bend chenille stems into shapes to represent the three men and the angel of the Lord. Glue or staple them to the bulletin board.

Other Ideas

1. Omit chenille stems and draw the figures instead.
2. Use liquid starch to attach crepe paper to the background.
3. Use colored tissue paper instead of crepe paper.

RESCUED BY THE LORD

Bible Story

Daniel in the lions' den. Daniel 6

Materials

Light-colored paper
Paper plates
Yarn in assorted colors
Scissors
Glue
Stapler
Pencils
Construction paper scraps
Ruler

Teacher Preparation

1. Cut paper to fit the bulletin board.
2. Cut yarn into 24" segments.
3. Provide yarn, scissors, paper plates, pencils, paper scraps, and glue.
4. Have a stapler ready to use.

Classroom Activity

1. Print the letters for the title "Rescued by the Lord" on the paper. Glue yarn to outline the letters.
2. When the glue is dry, attach the paper to the bulletin board.
3. Give each child a paper plate. Cut and glue yarn on the back of the paper plates to make lions' manes. Use paper cutouts for features such as eyes, nose, and mouth. Assign one child to make Daniel from a paper plate.
4. When the glue is dry, staple the paper plates to the board.
5. Talk about how God protected Daniel. Encourage students to share how God has protected them.

Other Ideas

1. Omit yarn. Instead draw features with markers or crayons.
2. Include a paper plate to represent King Darius. Add speech balloons for the conversation between him and Daniel in Daniel 6:19-22.

NEW TESTAMENT

GET READY FOR JESUS

Bible Story

The angel Gabriel appears to Mary. Luke 1:26-38

Materials

White paper
Cardboard tubes
Colorful wrapping paper
Green, red, and yellow tissue paper
Pencils
Scissors
Glue
Thumbtacks

Teacher Preparation

1. Cut white paper to fit the bulletin board.
2. Cut letters for title "Get Ready for Jesus" from wrapping paper.
3. Lightly draw an outline of an Advent wreath on the paper. Use an overhead projector to enlarge the outline on page 55. (Older children can cut out letters and draw the wreath themselves.)
4. Cut 2" tissue paper squares. The number of squares needed will depend on the size of your bulletin board. Cut green squares for the wreath, red for berries, and yellow for the flames.
5. Provide cardboard tubes, wrapping paper, scissors, and glue.

Classroom Activity

1. Share ways that we, like Mary, get ready for the birth of Jesus at Christmastime. Explain how the wreath we will make for our bulletin board will help us mark the four weeks before Christmas that we call Advent.
2. Cut the cardboard tubes to the sizes you need. Cut wrapping paper and glue it around the tubes. Tack them to the wreath.
3. Twist each green tissue paper square around the eraser end of a pencil and glue it to the wreath. Crumple the red squares into balls and glue them around the wreath.
4. Each week, twist and glue on yellow squares to "light" a candle.

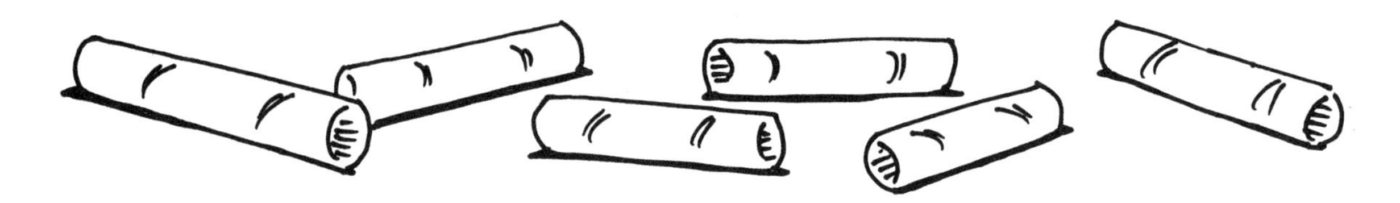

WREATH PATTERN

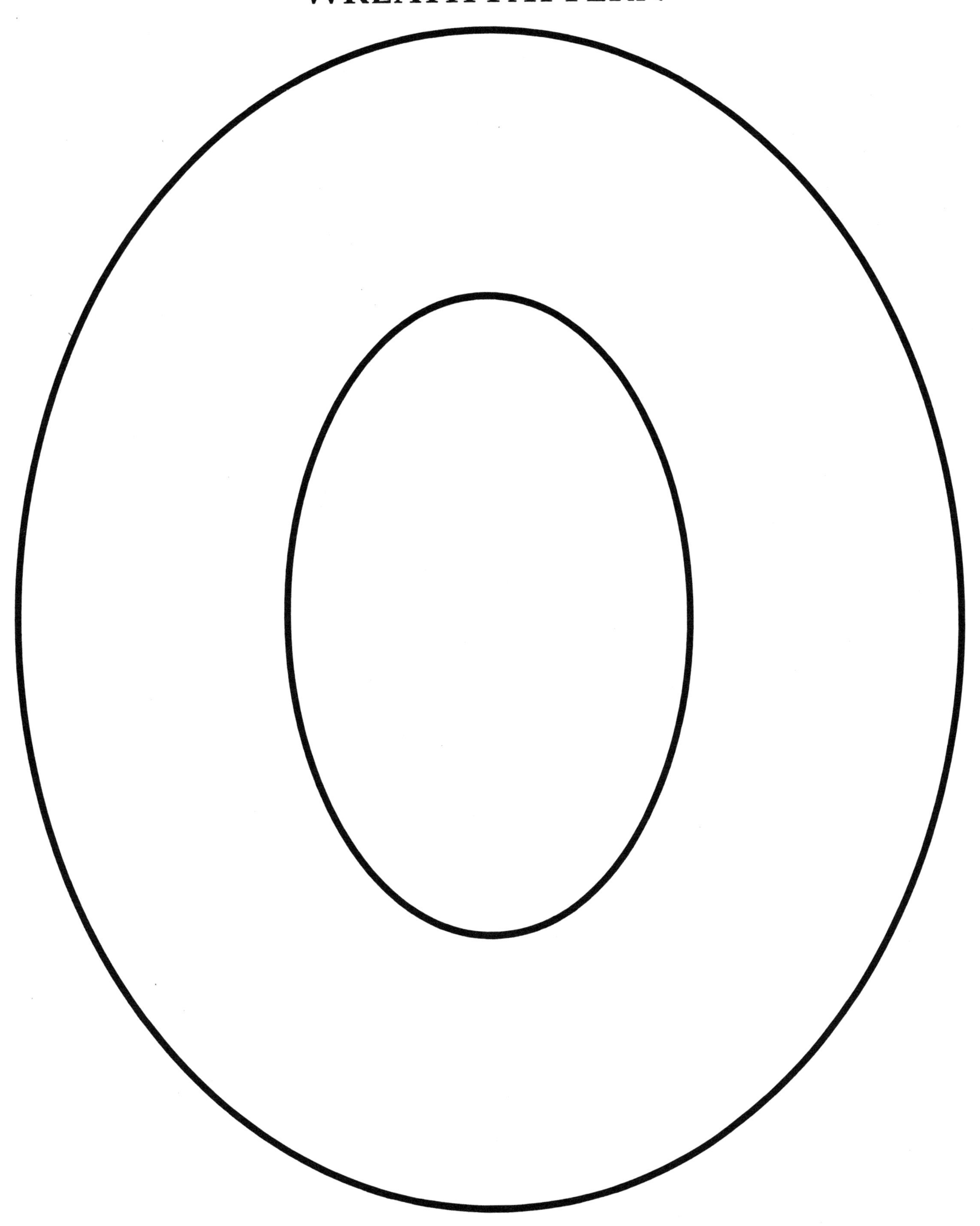

THE ROAD TO BETHLEHEM

Bible Story

Mary and Joseph go to Bethlehem. Luke 2:1-5

Materials

Green and tan paper
White drawing paper
Construction paper
Pencil
Markers
Scissors
Stapler
Glue
Ruler

Teacher Preparation

1. Cut green paper to fit the bulletin board. Cut a tan strip of paper to represent a winding road going the width of the bulletin board.
2. Draw and cut out construction paper outlines of Mary, Joseph, and Bethlehem. Enlarge the patterns on page 57. Cut letters for the title "On the Way to Bethlehem" from construction paper. (Older children can cut the letters themselves.)
3. Cut 25 white 4" x 4" paper squares.
4. Duplicate and cut apart the biblical references on page 58.
5. Have a stapler ready to use.
6. Provide construction paper, scissors, markers, and glue.

Classroom Activity

1. Glue the road, Mary, Joseph, and Bethlehem to the green paper.
2. Attach the paper to the bulletin board.
3. Divide biblical references among members of the class. Glue each reference to a white paper square. Use a marker to draw the part of the Christmas story each reference describes.
4. Trace and cut out a square of construction paper for each biblical reference. Write the number for each reference on the square as illustrated.
5. Glue the white square to the poster paper. Help students staple each construction paper square over a white square at the top.

5. Mary and Joseph had to travel the long road from Nazareth to Bethlehem before Jesus was born. Use this bulletin board for an Advent calendar to help students go on an imaginary journey to Bethlehem. Pull a square off for each day in December. As you do so, read or tell the connection between the symbol and the Christmas story. When you get to 25, you will be there–it will be Christmas day!

Other Ideas

1. Instead of biblical references, draw Christmas symbols on the bulletin board.
2. On the white squares write Old Testament prophecies or passages from the Gospels about Jesus' birth.
3. Draw a tree outline on the bulletin board. Cut round symbols to be uncovered during the days before Advent.

MARY, JOSEPH, AND BETHLEHEM PATTERNS

BIBLICAL REFERENCES FOR "THE ROAD TO BETHLEHEM"

1. Zechariah burns incense in the temple. Luke 1:5-10
2. An angel appears to Zechariah. Luke 1:11-20
3. Zechariah cannot speak to the people. Luke 1:21-23
4. The angel Gabriel appears to Mary. Luke 1:26-38
5. Mary visits Elizabeth. Luke 1:39-45
6. Mary praises God. Luke 1:46-55
7. An angel appears to Joseph. Matthew 1:18-25
8. John the Baptist is born. Luke 1:57-66
9. Zechariah praises God. Luke 1:67-79
10. Caesar Augustus issues a decree. Luke 2:1-2
11. Joseph and Mary go to Bethlehem. Luke 2:4-5
12. There is no room in the inn. Luke 2:7
13. Jesus is born in Bethlehem. Luke 2:6-7
14. Jesus lies in a manger. Luke 2:7
15. An angel appears to the shepherds. Luke 2:8-12
16. Many angels appear in the sky. Luke 2:13-14
17. The shepherds see Baby Jesus. Luke 2:15-16
18. The shepherds tell others about Jesus. Luke 2:17-18
19. The new baby is named "Jesus." Luke 2:21
20. Wise men follow a star. Matthew 2:1-2
21. Wise men talk to Herod. Matthew 2:1-8
22. Wise men follow the star to Bethlehem. Matthew 2:9-10
23. Some wise men worship Jesus. Matthew 2:11
24. Wise men give their gifts to Jesus. Matthew 2:11
25. Celebrate Jesus' birth–today is Christmas day!

OH LITTLE TOWN OF BETHLEHEM

Bible Story

Jesus is born in Bethlehem. Luke 2:4-7

Materials

Blue paper
Black and yellow construction paper
Scissors
Glue
Glitter
Black markers

Teacher Preparation

1. Cut blue paper to fit the bulletin board.
2. From yellow construction paper, cut letters for the title "Oh Little Town of Bethlehem" as well as an outline of a stable.
3. Cut squares and rectangles from black construction paper. (Older children can cut letters and shapes themselves.)
4. Provide glitter, markers, and glue.

Classroom Activity

1. Talk about how Jesus' birth in Bethlehem fulfilled Old Testament prophecies.
2. Glue pieces of black construction paper to the paper to make an outline of Bethlehem. Glue the yellow stable in the center of the Bethlehem outline.
3. Use the black marker to draw the outline of a manger in the center of the yellow stable piece, as well as to add other details.
4. Draw stars in the sky with glue; sprinkle them with glitter. Draw the largest star over the stable.
5. Glue the title to the top of the paper.
6. Attach the paper to the bulletin board.

Other Ideas

1. Write the title, "Oh Little Town of Bethlehem," with colored glitter.
2. Cut out a black manger outline to glue on the stable piece.
3. Cut the Bethlehem skyline from one long piece of black paper.

COME LET US ADORE HIM

Bible Story

Birth of Jesus. Luke 2:6-7

Materials

White paper
Corrugated cardboard
Stapler
Metallic ribbon
Saucer
Markers or crayons
Colored construction paper
Scissors
Glue
Ruler

Teacher Preparation

1. Attach paper to the bulletin board.
2. Cut one V-shaped piece and two long rectangles from corrugated cardboard. Staple the pieces together on the bulletin board to make a manger. (Older children can do the cutting themselves.)
3. Trace around a saucer on construction paper to make a circle. Make one to represent each child in your class. Make an additional circle to represent Baby Jesus and cut it in half.
4. Have a stapler ready to use.
5. Outline letters for the title "Oh Come Let Us Adore Him" on the paper. (Older children can do this themselves.)
6 Cut metalic ribbon into 24" lengths.
7. Provide construction paper, scissors, glue, and markers or crayons.

Classroom Activity

1. Draw features to represent a sleeping baby on the half circle, and staple it on top of the manger.
2. Cut metalic ribbon into small pieces. Glue them on the bulletin board to look like straw in the manger. Decorate the title with metalic ribbon too.
3. Let each child choose a circle to match his skin color and draw his own face on it. Construction paper details may be added. Staple the circles to the bulletin board as a reminder to praise Jesus this Christmas season.

JOY TO THE WORLD

Bible Story

Angels appear to shepherds. Luke 2:8-20

Materials

Dark blue or black paper
Paper lace doilies
White tissue paper
Round suckers on sticks
Yarn
Thumbtacks
Glue
Markers
Pencils
Ruler
Scissors

Teacher Preparation

1. Cut paper to fit the bulletin board.
2. Outline letters for the title "Joy to the World" on the paper. Enlarge the letters on page 62. (Older children can trace letters themselves.)
3. Cut a half circle from each doily for each angel.
4. Cut several of the doilies into small pieces.
5. Cut yarn into 6" segments.
6. Provide suckers, white tissue paper, yarn, markers, and glue. Have thumbtacks ready to use.

Classroom Activity

1. Glue small pieces of doily inside the title, "Joy to the World." Let the letters dry, then attach the paper to the bulletin board.
2. Make an angel by placing a sucker in the middle of a tissue square, and tying yarn around the stick with a knot and a loop at the base of the sucker.
3. Glue the doily half circle to the back of the angel for wings.
4. If you wish, add yarn hair, eyes, and a mouth to the angel.
5. After several angels are made, attach them to the bulletin board, using a thumbtack through the yarn loop.
6. Join the angel choir. Sing "Joy to the World" and other Christmas songs.

Other Ideas

1. Pleat tissue and attach it to a circle for a head.
2. Add pieces of metallic ribbon to fill in the title.
3. Use metallic garland to outline the title.
4. Make the angels' wings and bodies from doilies.

BULLETIN BOARD TITLE

WISE MEN STILL SEEK HIM

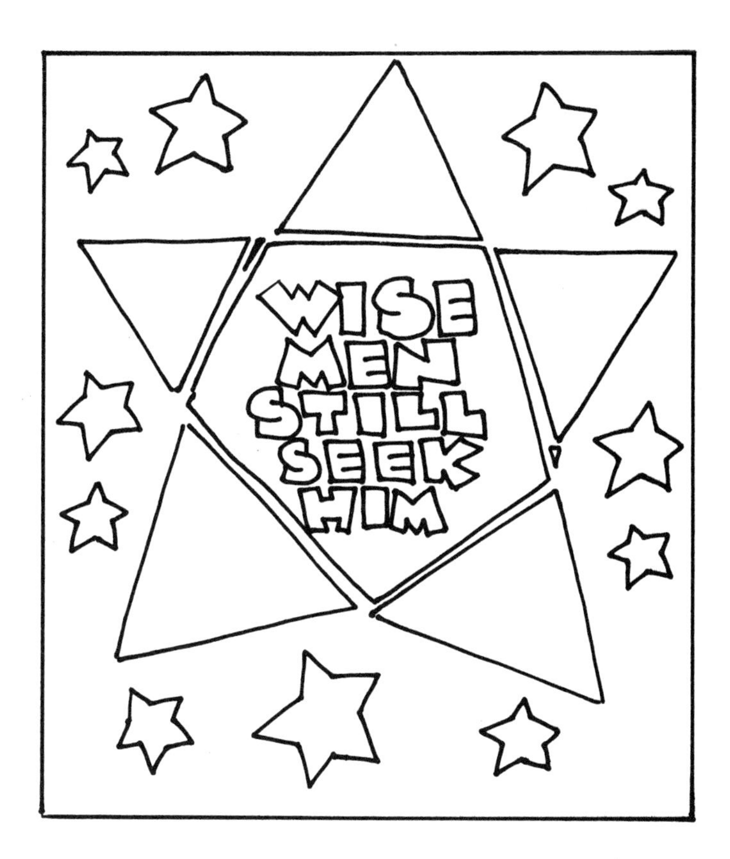

Bible Story

Wise men come to see Jesus.
Matthew 2:1-12

Materials

Dark blue paper
Yellow poster board
Pencil
Yarn
Metallic wrapping paper (different patterns)
Glue
Scissors
Glitter marker or pen
Tracing paper
Stapler
Ruler

Teacher Preparation

1. Cut blue paper to fit the bulletin board.
2. Cut yarn into 24" segments.
3. Cut wrapping paper into squares.
4. Lightly outline and cut out a star from yellow poster board. Use an overhead projector to enlarge the star on page 64. Trace the title "Wise Men Still Seek Him" inside the star. (Older children can do this themselves.)
5. Provide glue, scissors, pencils, tracing paper, and glitter marker or pen.
6. Have a stapler ready to use.

Classroom Activity

1. Glue yarn around the star outline.
2. Assign someone to go over the letters in the title with a glitter marker or pen.
3. Attach the paper to the board.
4. Assign a section of the star to different children. Have the children fill in the five sections with different pieces of metallic wrapping paper. (Trace over the outline with tracing paper, cut out the shape, then trace it on metallic paper. Cut out the shapes and glue them in the sections on the poster board star.)
5. Staple the poster board star to the bulletin board.
6. Let each child cut a small star from metallic paper and glue a yarn outline around it. When it's dry, staple the star to the bulletin board.

7. Long ago a bright star led the wise men to Jesus. Let this bulletin board remind us that "wise men" still seek Jesus today.

Other Ideas

1. Cut out wrapping paper stars to outline with yarn.
2. Cut stars from poster board, cover them with different colors of foil, and hang them with string from the bulletin board.

STAR PATTERN

NEWS OF GREAT JOY

Bible Story

The Christmas story. Luke 2:4-12;
Matthew 1:16-21

Materials

White paper
Christmas cookie cutters
Tempera paint
Paintbrushes
Paper towels
Paper plates
Scissors
Detergent
Newspapers
Pencil

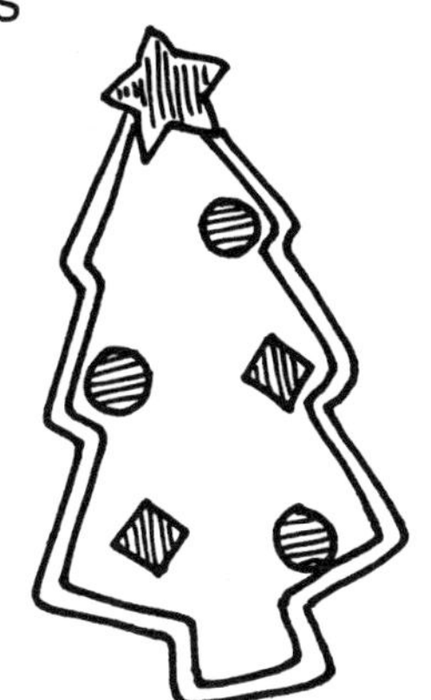

Teacher Preparation

1. A week before the project, send a note home with the students requesting Christmas cookie cutters such as stars, camels, and angels.
2. Cut paper to fit the bulletin board. Place paper on a newspaper covered work area.
3. Outline the title "Good News for All People" on the paper. (Older children can do this themselves.)
4. For each tempera color you use, place two folded paper towels on a paper plate. Pour paint on the plates to make stamp pads. Add a few drops of detergent to each plate to aid in cleanup.
5. Provide Christmas cookie cutters, paint, and paintbrushes.

Classroom Activity

1. Paint the title, "Good News for All People," on the paper. Talk about why Jesus is "Good News" for us today.
2. Dip cookie cutters in the paper plate stamp pads and stamp them on the paper. Talk about the significance of the figures.
3. When the paper is dry, attach it to the bulletin board.

Other Ideas

1. Add glitter to wet tempera.
2. Stamp shapes on a Christmas tree outline.

HOW JESUS LIVED

Bible Story

Jesus grows up in Nazareth.
Luke 2:39-40

Materials

White paper
Book on life in Bible times
Construction paper
White drawing paper
Markers, crayons, or colored pencils
Yarn
Glue
Scissors
Yardstick

Teacher Preparation

1. Attach white paper to the bulletin board.
2. Draw a line down the middle of the paper. Write "Life in Jesus' Time" on one half of the paper and "Life in Our Times" on the other. (Older children can do this themselves.)
3. Bring to class a book showing pictures of life in Bible times.
4. Cut yarn into 36" segments.
5. Provide construction paper, glue, and markers, colored pencils, or crayons.

Classroom Activity

1. Look at pictures from a book of life in Bible times to see how Jesus lived. Talk about things He did that are different from what we do now. Look for pictures of things that Jesus may have seen or used as a boy.
2. Draw "then and now" pictures on separate sheets of drawing paper to show how people lived in Bible times and how they live now. Glue the pictures on larger pieces of construction paper.
3. Glue appropriate pictures across from each other on the board.
4. Glue a piece of yarn between each "then and now" picture to connect them.

Other Ideas

1. Draw pictures directly on the white paper.
2. In the center of the board draw a picture of Jesus as a boy surrounded by things He may have used.
3. Discuss the things we have in common with Bible time families: eating, sleeping, working, celebrating, learning, etc.

LIKE A DOVE

Bible Story

The baptism of Jesus. Matthew 3:13-17

Materials

Blue paper
White poster board
Styrofoam™ pieces (used in packing)
Glue
Pencils
Scissors
Light blue construction paper
Stapler

Teacher Preparation

1. Attach blue paper to the bulletin board.
2. Cut letters from white poster board for the title "God's Spirit Came Down."
3. Draw a dove shape on the white poster board and cut it out. Use an overhead projector to enlarge the pattern on page 68. (Older children can cut the letters and dove themselves.)
4. Provide light blue construction paper, pencils, scissors, Styrofoam™ pieces, and glue.
5. Have the stapler ready to use.

Classroom Activity

1. Glue the Styrofoam™ pieces to the dove shape.
2. Staple the dove and letters to the board.
3. Give each child a piece of light blue construction paper from which to cut the shape of a drop of water. Glue the water drops to the board.
4. Review what happened when Jesus was baptized and God's Spirit came down like a dove from heaven. Talk about how people are baptized in your church.

Other Ideas

1. Cover the dove with whipped soap instead of Styrofoam™ pieces.
2. Omit Styrofoam™ pieces on the dove. Instead, cover it with white feathers.
3. If children in your class have been baptized, have them write their names and baptismal date on the drops of water.

DOVE PATTERN

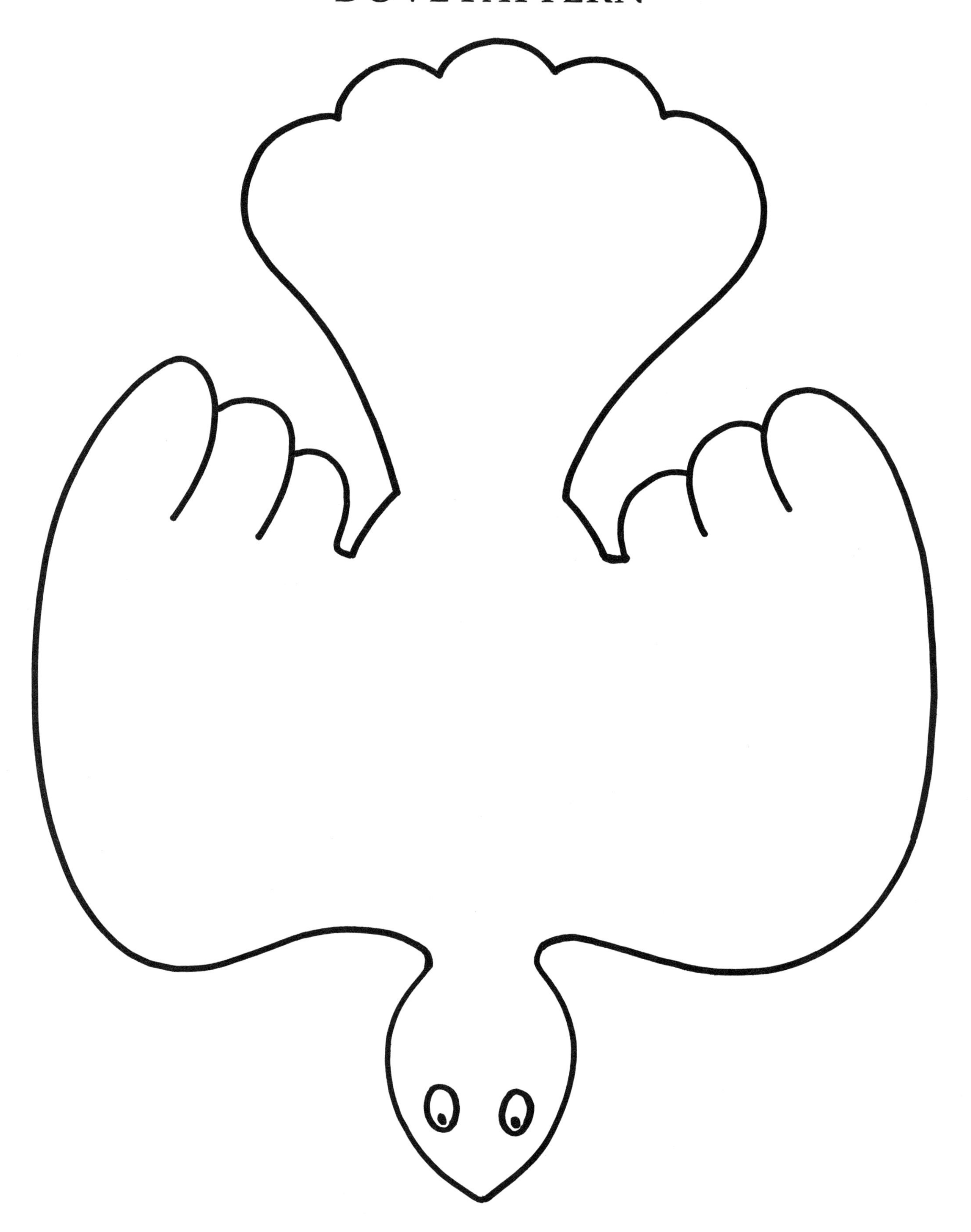

FOLLOWING THE LORD

Bible Story

The calling of the first disciples.

Matthew 4:18-22

Materials

Brown paper
Construction paper
Crayons
Scissors
Glue

Teacher Preparation

1. Cover the bulletin board with brown paper.
2. Cut out large construction paper letters for the title "Follow the Lord." (Older children can draw and cut out the letters themselves.)
3. Provide construction paper, scissors, crayons, and glue.

Classroom Activity

1. Cut out a large sandal shape. Add details and write "Jesus" on it.
2. Let each child choose a piece of construction paper the color of his shoes. Trace one shoe and write the student's name on it. Add details; then cut it out.
3. Color designs on the letters of the title.
4. Glue the title across the middle of the board with Jesus' sandal to the right of it.
5. Glue the children's shoes on the board, following in the same direction as Jesus' sandal. Talk about ways we can follow Jesus.

Other Ideas

1. Trace shoes directly on the paper.
2. Stamp souls of shoes instead, using tempera mixed with detergent for easier cleanup. Cut out and attach to bulletin board.
3. Stamp footprints on construction paper. Wash feet with soap and water. Attach footprints to bulletin board.

TWELVE WHO WERE SENT

Bible Story

The twelve disciples. Matthew 10:1-4

Materials

White paper
12 paper lunch bags
Markers
Construction paper
Glue
Scissors
Newspaper
Thumbtacks
Rubber bands

Teacher Preparation

1. Attach white paper to the bulletin board.
2. Cut construction paper letters for the title "Called to Follow." (Older children can do this themselves.)
3. Provide newspaper, construction paper, scissors, paper bags, rubber bands, glue, markers, and thumbtacks.

Classroom Activity

1. Glue letters for the title, "Called to Follow," on the board.
2. Divide the names of the twelve disciples among the class. Have each child, or group of children, use a paper bag to make a puppet head representing a disciple.
3. Use markers or construction paper cutouts to make facial features and hair.
4. After decorating the bag, stuff it with newspaper. Use a rubber band to fasten the bag. Tack the puppets to the bulletin board.
5. Write the names of the disciples under the bags.
6. Take turns telling about each disciple.

GIVE TO THE LORD

Bible Story

The widow's offering. Luke 21:1-4

Materials

White paper
Construction paper (yellow and other colors)
Cardboard
Foil (aluminum or colored)
Glue
Scissors
Markers

Teacher Preparation

1. Attach white paper to the bulletin board.
2. Cut small cardboard circles, the size of coins.
3. Cut construction paper letters for the title "Give to the Lord."
4. Draw and cut out an outline of a large collection plate from yellow construction paper. Use an overhead projector to enlarge the pattern on page 72. Glue the collection plate on the board. (Older children can cut the letters for the title and the plate themselves.)
5. Provide foil, scissors, construction paper, markers, and glue.

Classroom Activity

1. Glue letters for the title, "Give to the Lord," to the bulletin board.
2. Cover cardboard circles with foil to look like coins. Glue them on the board in and above the offering plate.
3. The widow gave money to the Lord. What can we give Him? (Talents, time, clothes for a church welfare program, canned goods for a food pantry.) Let each child cut a circle from construction paper, then draw a picture or write the name of something special she can give the Lord. Glue everyone's circle to the board.

Other Ideas

1. Cut collection plate and letters from yellow foil.
2. Cut out a collection plate and an offering jar, like the kind used in Jesus' story. Write "Then" over the jar and "Now" over the collection plate.
3. Draw a picture of the woman giving her two coins on one side of the bulletin board, and a boy and girl placing money into a collection plate on the other side.
4. Outline the plate and fill it with crayon coin rubbings.

OFFERING PLATE PATTERN

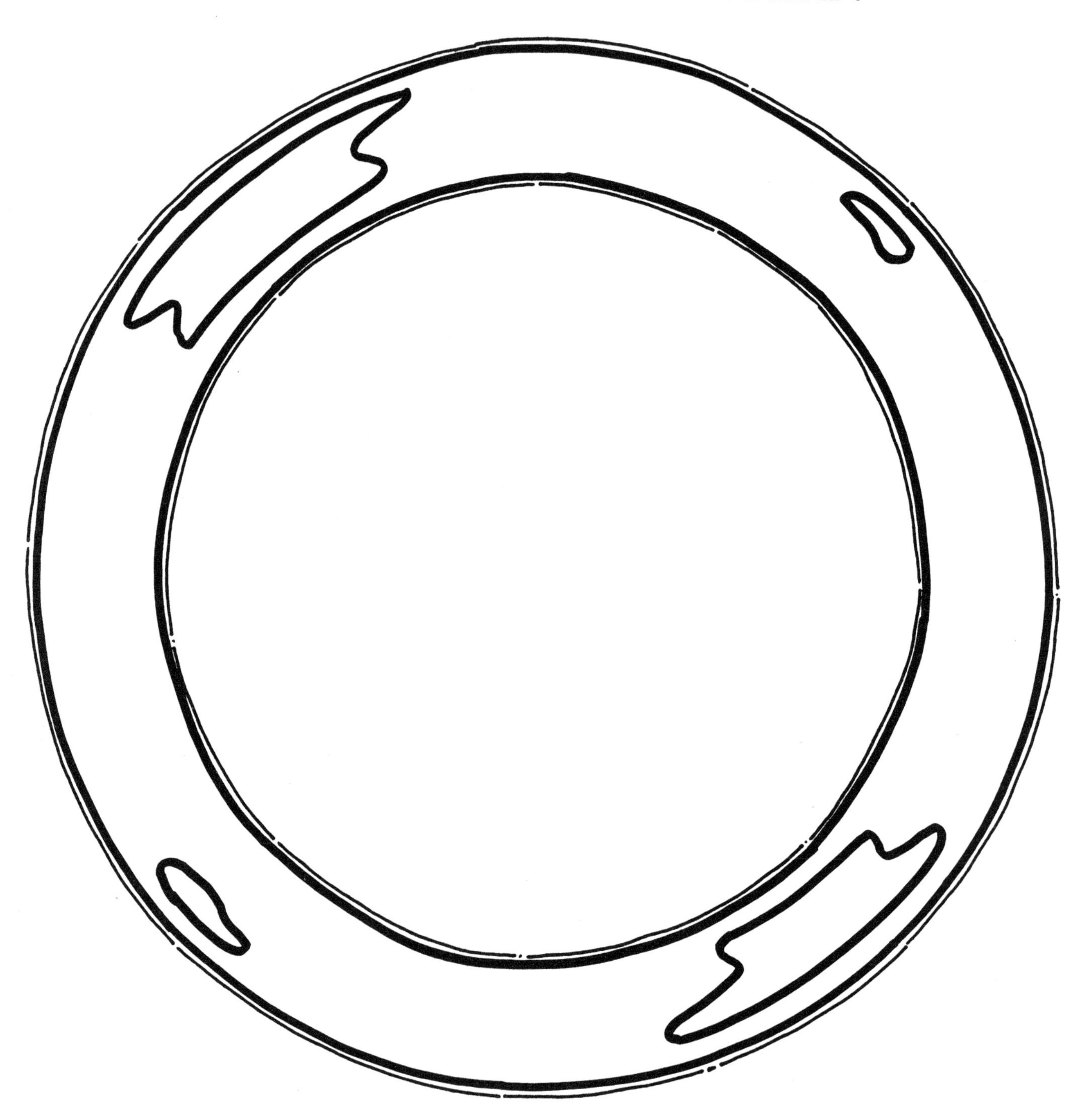

THE WINDS AND WAVES OBEY HIM

Bible Story

Jesus stills the storm.
Matthew 8:23-27

Materials

White paper
Blue and gray finger paints
Cookie sheet
Paper
Markers
Scissors
Newspapers

Teacher Preparation

1. Cut white paper to fit the bulletin board. Place paper on newspapers in work area.
2. Write the title "The Winds and the Waves Obey Him" at the top of the paper, and draw a line down the middle.
3. Draw and cut out the outline of a sailboat. Use an overhead projector to enlarge the boat on page 74. (Children can cut out the boats and draw patterns for the lettering themselves.) You will need two boats.
4. Pour paint on a cookie sheet.
5. Provide markers.

Classroom Activity

1. Talk about how the Sea of Galilee must have looked before and after Jesus told the waves to be still. What would it have felt like to be one of the disciples at that time?
2. Take turns finger painting waves in the calm water and wild waves in the storm.
3. When the paint is dry, put the boat in each scene. Draw Jesus sleeping in the first boat and standing in the second.

Other Ideas

1. Make only the stormy sea with Jesus telling it to be still.
2. Use whipped soap to make the waves look more realistic.

BOAT PATTERN

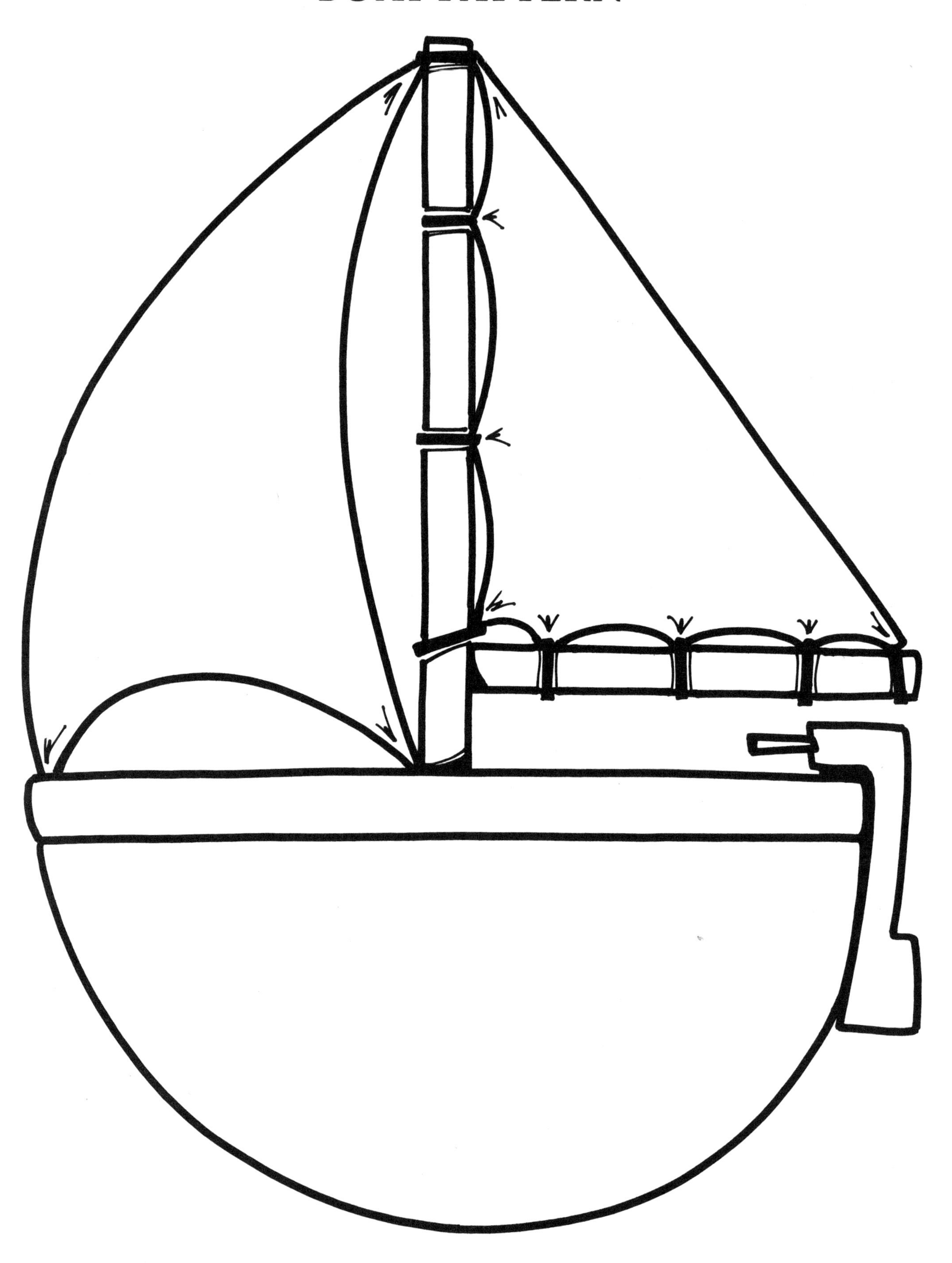

ALIVE IN CHRIST

Bible Story

Raising of a widow's son. Luke 7:11-17

Materials

Wrapping paper
Construction paper
Scissors
Pencils
Glue
Markers (optional)

Teacher Preparation

1. Cover the bulletin board with wrapping paper.
2. Cut construction paper letters for the title "Alive in Christ." (Older children can do this themselves.)
3. Make an example of symmetrical cutting of a person with hands held high. To do this, fold a piece of construction paper in half. Along the fold, lightly sketch an outline of half a person. Cut it out, then unfold it.
4. Provide construction paper, pencils, and glue.

Classroom Activity

1. Glue the title to the bulletin board.
2. After demonstrating symmetrical cutting, encourage children to cut out their own figures. Each student may write his name on his cutout figure.
3. Glue the figures on the board. Jesus gave the young man new life–talk about how He gives new life to us.

Other Ideas

1. Draw a face and other details on each cutout figure.
2. Use a solid color background and draw patterns on the letters of the title.

JESUS LOVES ME

Bible Story

Jesus and the children.
Matthew 19:13-15

Materials

Fabric scraps
Pinking shears
Colored glue
Stapler

Teacher Preparation

1. Cut fabric scraps into squares. Size will depend on the number of members in the class and the size of your bulletin board. Make a square for each class member plus one for the center square. Cut additional squares as needed to fill the bulletin board. To provide contrast, use one color for the "name" squares and a contrasting color for the fill-in squares.
2. Write "Jesus Loves Me" on one square. (Older children can do this themselves.) Staple the square at the center of the board.
3. Provide colored glue.
4. Have a stapler ready to use.

Classroom Activity

1. Let each child write his name with colored glue on a square.
2. Encourage the children to work out a pattern for the squares on the bulletin board.
3. Staple the squares to the board.
4. Let this "quilt" be a reminder that Jesus loves each of us and wants us to come to Him like the children who came to Him in the Bible story.

Other Ideas

1. Draw names on the squares with markers instead of colored glue.
2. Sew the squares together on a sewing machine.
3. Glue squares to a piece of paper or poster board.
4. Cut squares from construction paper instead of cloth.
5. Draw a picture of Jesus and the children on the center square. Have each child add his picture and name to his square.

OH GIVE THANKS

Bible Story

Feeding the five thousand.
Mark 6:30-44

Materials

White paper
Scissors
Tempera paints
Paper plates
Paper towels
Different kinds of vegetables (corn, cucumbers, potatoes, carrots, broccoli, mushrooms, etc.)
Knife
Pencil
Newspaper
Rinse water in a dish
Detergent

Teacher Preparation

1. Cut white paper to fit the bulletin board. Place paper on newspapers in work area.
2. Lightly sketch the title "Oh Give Thanks" on the paper. Use an overhead projector to enlarge the title on page 78. (Older children can do this themselves.)
3. Fold two paper towels and place them on a paper plate for each color of tempera you plan to use. Pour the tempera on the plates to make stamp pads. Add a little detergent to aid in cleanup.
4. Provide a variety of vegetables that are firm enough to stamp a clear pattern. Cut each in half.
5. Provide rinse water in a dish as well as extra paper towels.

Classroom Activity

1. Dip vegetables into tempera and stamp them on the paper. Stamp the letters of the title with a distinctive vegetable or color.
2. When the paper is dry, attach it to the board.
3. Talk about how Jesus gave thanks before feeding the people. Take turns thanking God for a favorite food.

Other Ideas

1. Stamp vegetables on a large paper plate drawn on the bulletin board or on a real paper plate
2. Cut construction paper outlines of favorite foods to glue on the board.
3. Write individual meal prayers on sheets of paper, and glue them to a larger sheet of construction paper. Stamp a vegetable design around the sheet for a border, then put it on the bulletin board.

BULLETIN BOARD TITLE

JESUS' LITTLE LAMB

Bible Story

The parable of the lost sheep.
Matthew 18:10-14

Materials

Light blue paper
White and green construction paper
Pencil
Scissors
Glue
Stapler
Ruler

Teacher Preparation

1. Attach blue paper to the bulletin board.
2. Cut green construction paper into 4" strips.
3. Cut letters for the title "I Am Jesus' Little Lamb" from green construction paper.
4. Draw and cut out a lamb from white paper. Use an overhead projector to enlarge the lamb on page 80. (Older children can cut the letters and lamb themselves.)
5. Cut strips of white paper 1" wide.
6. Cut a small circle of blue paper for the lamb's eye.
7. Provide scissors and glue.
8. Have a stapler ready to use.

Classroom Activity

1. Glue the title at the top of the bulletin board.
2. Cut strips of white paper 1" x 3". Use scissors to curl the strips.
3. Glue curled strips to the lamb to look like wool.
4. Glue the eye on the lamb.
5. Fringe strips of green paper for grass. You may want to curl the grass too.
6. Glue strips of green paper across the bottom of the board.
7. Staple the lamb to the board.
8. Jesus told the story of the lost sheep to show how much God loves each of His little ones. Read the story Jesus told and talk about how it makes us feel to know that God cares so much for us.

Other Ideas

1. Glue cotton or curled, white ribbon on the lamb.
2. Sing "I Am Jesus' Little Lamb" or another song emphasizing that God loves us, like a shepherd loves his sheep.
3. Curl strips of grass, or cut individual pieces of grass to glue to the bulletin board.
4. Add construction paper flowers and clouds to the board.
5. Use flowered fabric for the grass and lettering.

LAMB PATTERN

GROW IN GOD'S LOVE

Bible Story

Parable of the Good Samaritan.
Luke 10:25-37

Materials

Light blue paper
Construction paper (green, pink, red, and purple)
Scissors
Glue
Pencils
Ruler

Teacher Preparation

1. Attach blue paper to the bulletin board.
2. Cut 6" strips of green construction paper the length of the bulletin board for grass.
3. Cut construction paper letters for the title "Grow in God's Love." (Older children can cut out the letters themselves.)
4. Demonstrate symmetrical heart cutting. Fold a piece of paper in half and lightly draw half a heart on the fold. Cut and unfold. Cut a second time to show how repeated cuts can be made to have a heart within a heart. (See illustration.)
5. Cut different sizes of pink, red, and purple squares. Cut smaller green squares.
6. Provide construction paper, scissors, pencils, and glue.

Classroom Activity

1. Glue the title to the top of the bulletin board.
2. Fringe grass and glue to bottom of board.
3. Cut strips of green paper for stems.
4. With the teacher's example as a guide; fold, outline, and cut out green hearts for leaves. Fold, outline, and cut out red, pink, and purple hearts for flowers. Cut large hearts into several concentric smaller ones.
5. Glue hearts to the bulletin board, using both concentric and solid hearts. Use the hearts to make different kinds of flowers.
6. Glue stems and heart-shaped leaves on the board.
7. Talk about ways we can, like the Good Samaritan, demonstrate God's love to others.

Other Ideas

1. Use a burlap background. Cut hearts, leaves, stems, and grass from fabric scraps.
2. Use colored tissue paper instead of construction paper. Attach the pieces with rubber cement.
3. Print each student's name on the stem of the heart flower she made.
4. Cut paper cups in half and fasten them to the bottom of the flower stems for flowerpots.
5. Optional: Use an overhead projector to enlarge the heart below to place in the center of the bulletin board.

HEART PATTERN

THE SEED ON GOOD SOIL

Bible Story

The parable of the sower. Luke 8:4-15

Materials

Striped wallpaper
Potatoes
Knife
Markers
Orange tempera paint
2 paper towels
Paper plate
Masking tape
Scissors

Teacher Preparation

1. Cut enough striped wallpaper to cover the bulletin board.
2. Write the title "The Seed on Good Soil" on the wallpaper. (Older children can do this themselves.)
3. Cut potatoes in half. Cut the outline of a head of grain in each half potato as shown.
4. Place two paper towels on a paper plate. Pour tempera paint on the plate to make a stamp pad.

Classroom Activity

1. Dip the potato half in the paint and stamp it on the bulletin board, keeping the grain head pattern vertical with the stripes. Fill the bulletin board with the stamps. Let it dry.
2. The seed in Jesus' story was the Word of God. What are some of the ways we can become better soil in which God's Word can grow?

Other Ideas

1. Instead of potato prints, glue pasta or yarn on the board to represent grain.
2. Use plain paper for the background and attach construction paper grain to the bulletin board.

GOD CARES FOR ME

Bible Story

The flowers of the field. Matthew 6:28-34

Materials

Light blue paper
Colored tissue paper
Stapler
Green chenille stems
Green floral or plastic tape
Scissors

Teacher Preparation

1. Attach blue paper to the bulletin board.
2. Bend chenille stems to form letters for the title "God Cares for Me." (Older students can do this themselves.) Staple chenille stem letters to the bulletin board.
3. Cut long strips of tissue paper, double the width you want the flowers to be. Fold the strips in half. (Cut one strip for every child in the class.)
4. Provide chenille stems and green tape.
5. Have a stapler ready to use.

Classroom Activity

1. Have each child choose a tissue strip to make into a flower. Roll the folded tissue strip around the end of a chenille stem gathering the bottom together as you do so. Tape the gathered bottom of the flower to the chenille stem as shown.
2. Staple the flowers to the board.
3. Add green tissue paper grass to the bottom of the board.

Other Ideas

1. Cut and glue flat tissue flowers and lettering to white paper.
2. Make flowers from construction paper.
3. Experiment with different ways to make tissue paper flowers.
4. Use flowers for an Easter garden.

TRUST IN THE LORD

Bible Story

The birds of the air. Matthew 6:25-27

Materials

Light blue paper
Construction paper (assorted colors)
Scissors
Glue
Birdseed (or raw rice) in a bowl
Stapler
Markers

Teacher Preparation

1. Check out a bird book from a library to show the class.
2. Attach blue paper to the bulletin board.
3. Cut a piece of construction paper for each letter of the title "Trust in the Lord." Outline the letters. (Older children can do this themselves.)
4. Provide birdseed, construction paper, scissors, markers, and glue.
5. Have a stapler ready to use.

Classroom Activity

1. Read Jesus' words about God's care for birds. Look at pictures of birds and talk about the variety of birds created and cared for by God. Remind students that God takes care of us even better than He takes care of the birds.
2. Divide the letters in the title, "Trust in the Lord," among the class. Each child or pair of children draws his letter on a piece of construction paper. Cover the letter with glue, then with birdseed. When it's dry, staple the letters to the center of the board.
3. Have each child choose a bird he would like to make out of construction paper. Draw and cut out the body. Draw an eye and beak. Cut the wing separately and attach it with a fold at one end for a 3-D effect.
4. Staple or glue the birds to the bulletin board.

Other Ideas

1. Glue real feathers to the birds.
2. Use construction paper to make other foods eaten by birds such as worms, insects, and berries. Attach them to the bulletin board.

LET DOWN YOUR NET

Bible Story

The great catch of fish. John 21:1-14

Materials

Blue paper
Yellow tissue paper
Scissors
Construction paper
Newspaper
Stapler
Markers
Glue

Teacher Preparation

1. Attach blue paper to the bulletin board.
2. Cut letters for the title "Let Down Your Net" from construction paper.
3. Cut a net from tissue paper. (Older children can cut the letters for the title and the net themselves.)
   To make the net:
   a. Accordion fold a large sheet of tissue paper.
   b. Cut alternating slits down the folded strip as shown.
   c. Unfold carefully and staple the net to the bulletin board.
   d. Cut additional nets, enough to cover the bulletin board.
4. Provide scissors, construction paper, glue, and newspaper.
5. Have a stapler ready to use.

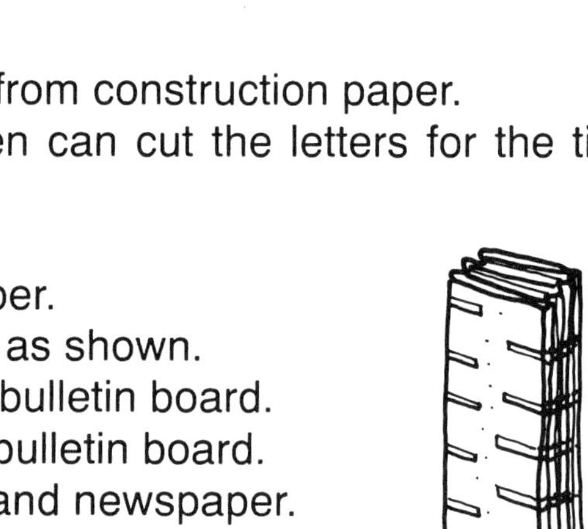

Classroom Activity

1. Each child should cut two pieces of construction paper for each fish, and staple them together, leaving the mouth open. Decorate one side with markers or construction paper cutouts, then stuff the fish with newspaper and staple the mouth shut. Staple the fish to the net on the board.
2. Glue letters for the title, "Let Down Your Net," at the top of the board. The words reminds us that, like the disciples, we should be "fishers of men," bringing them to Jesus.

Other Ideas

1. Make each fish from one piece of constuction paper.
2. Draw fish, net, and title with a crayon on white paper. Brush over them with a watercolor wash for an underwater effect.

GOD'S KINGDOM GROWS

Bible Story

The mustard seed. Matthew 13:31-32

Materials

White paper
Peeled crayons (green, brown, and assorted colors)
Mustard seed
Glue
Markers
Tree bark
Masking tape
Scissors

Teacher Preparation

1. Cut white paper to fit the bulletin board.
2. Ask each child to bring a leaf to class the day you will be making the bulletin board, or go outside together and find some.
3. Use markers to outline a tree with the words "God's Kingdom Grows" on its trunk. Use an overhead projector to enlarge the pattern on page 88. (Older children can outline the words and tree themselves.)
4. Provide bark, markers, mustard seed, glue, and peeled green and brown crayons. (If possible, have several color shades available.)

Classroom Activity

1. Take turns placing leaves under the tree outline and rubbing over them with green crayons. Place the bark under the tree trunk and rub over it lightly.
2. Outline letters in the title with bright-colored markers.
3. Glue the mustard seed at the bottom of the tree, or draw a dot to represent the seed.
4. Talk about Jesus' story of the mustard seed. God's kingdom grows from small beginnings. What can we do to help spread tiny seeds of God's love wherever we go?

Other Ideas

1. Glue pieces of torn tissue paper on the tree and the title.
2. Cut out leaf rubbings to glue on the tree.

TREE PATTERN

JESUS IS THE LIFE

Bible Story

Jesus and Lazarus. John 11:1-44

Materials

Yellow paper
Scissors
Construction paper
Glue
Hole punch
Shallow box
Pencil
Stapler
Markers

Teacher Preparation

1. Cut paper to fit the bulletin board.
2. Use markers to outline the title "Jesus Is the Life" on the paper. (Older children can do this themselves.)
3. Cut construction paper into different-sized rectangles.
4. Cut a sample of a symmetrical fold butterfly:
   a. Fold rectangle in half.
   b. Lightly outline half of butterfly with the body on the fold.
   c. Cut out the butterfly and unfold it. Fold up the wings on each side of the body.
5. Provide hole punch, glue, box, and construction paper scraps.
6. Have stapler ready to use.

Classroom Activity

1. Take turns punching holes out of construction paper scraps; place the dots in the box.
2. Glue dots inside the letters of the title.
3. Attach the paper to the bulletin board.
4. Draw and cut out a construction paper butterfly, using the symmetrical fold method. Don't forget to include the butterfly's body along the center fold.
5. Glue construction paper dots on the butterfly wings randomly or in patterns.
6. Partially fold up the butterfly wings. Staple everyone's butterfly to the bulletin board.

7. Review the story about Jesus raising Lazarus from the dead. Discuss how butterflies remind us of this story. The words on the board are from John 11:25-26. What does Jesus promise to all who believe in Him?

Other Ideas

1. Cover butterfly with torn or cut pieces of construction paper or tissue paper in a collage fashion.
2. Cut butterfly from two pieces of clear adhesive plastic and place pieces of tissue paper inside. Hang it from the top of the bulletin board.
3. Cut large circles for small children to glue to the butterfly wings.
4. Use gummed circles to cover butterflies and letters of title.
5. Use more of Jesus' words in John 11:25 for the title, such as "I am the resurrection and the life."
6. Enlarge the pattern below to make a butterfly for the bulletin board instead of or in addition to the children's individual butterflies.

BUTTERFLY PATTERN

HOSANNA

Bible Story

Jesus enters Jerusalem. Mark 11:1-11

Materials

White paper
Green construction paper
Markers
Scissors
Glue
Stapler

Teacher Preparation

1. Cut white paper to fit the bulletin board.
2. Draw large letters on the paper for the word "HOSANNA." Use an overhead projector to enlarge the letters on page 92. (Older children can outline the title themselves.)
3. Cut green construction paper into 1" wide strips.
4. Provide scissors, glue, and markers. Have a stapler ready to use.

Classroom Activity

1. Talk about the story of Jesus' triumphal entry into Jerusalem. How would it have felt to be one of the children shouting hosanna to Jesus as He passed?
2. Take turns decorating the letters with patterns. Attach the paper to the bulletin board.
3. Have each child cut a construction paper palm branch. Cut a long stem and short pieces to glue along the stem as shown. Glue the pieces together; then staple the palm leaf to the bulletin board.

Other Ideas

1. Decorate the letters with buttons, rickrack, sequins, plastic beads, and other decorative objects.
2. Paint the letters with florescent tempera paint and scatter drops of paint over the background.
3. Cut out solid leaf outlines and write "HOSANNA" on them. Try to make the letters show the happiness that comes from having Jesus as King.

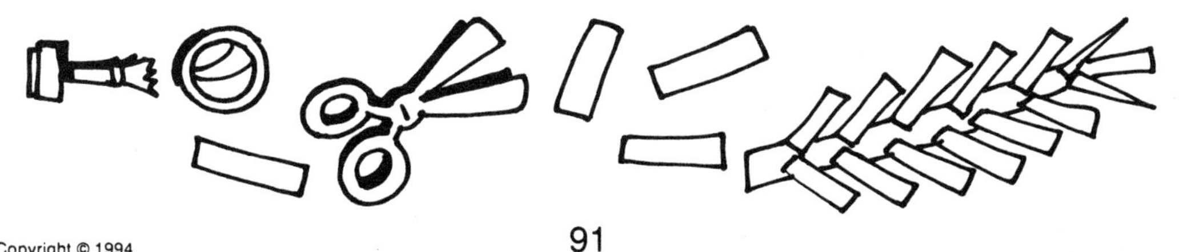

BULLETIN BOARD PATTERN

HE DIED FOR ALL

Bible Story

Jesus dies on the cross. John 19:16-37

Materials

White paper
Brown paper bags
Glue
Yardstick
Markers
Scissors
Pencil

Teacher Preparation

1. Cut white paper to fit the bulletin board.
2. Use a yardstick and pencil to draw a large cross on the paper.
3. Provide paper bags, markers, and glue.

Classroom Activity

1. Tear pieces from brown paper bags and glue them on the cross.
2. Draw people's faces around the cross. Each student may draw his family and himself.
3. Attach the paper to the board. Talk about how Jesus' death on the cross was for all people.
4. Write the title "He Died for All" on the cross.

Other Ideas

1. Glue purple pieces of paper for a Lenten cross and bright pieces for an Easter one.
2. Cut pictures from magazines to fill in the area behind the cross.

JESUS IS ALIVE

Bible Story

The empty tomb. John 20:1-18

Materials

White paper
Sunflower seeds
Construction paper (yellow and green)
Paper plates
Glue
Scissors
Pencils
Stapler

Teacher Preparation

1. Attach white paper to the bulletin board.
2. Cut strips of green construction paper for grass along the bottom of the board.
3. Cut yellow construction paper into 1" wide strips.
4. Provide glue, paper plates, seeds, scissors, and pencils.
5. Have a stapler ready to use.
6. Cut construction paper letters for the title "Jesus Is Alive." (Older children can do this themselves.)

Classroom Activity

1. Use scissors to fringe construction paper for grass. Staple the grass across the bottom of the board.
2. Give each child a paper plate.
3. Glue seeds in a circle at the center of each plate.
4. Cut the yellow construction paper strips into shorter segments (enough to go around the plate). Glue the yellow pieces around the plate for petals.
5. Staple the paper plates to the bulletin board.
6. Cut stems and leaves from green construction paper, and glue them on the flowers.
7. Talk about what happened when Jesus rose from the dead, and what His resurrection means to us today.

Other Ideas

1. Use twisted tissue paper to outline the letters at the top of the board.
2. Use construction paper to decorate paper plate flowers.

INTO ALL THE WORLD

Bible Story

The Great Commission.
Matthew 28:16-20

Materials

Blue paper
Construction paper
Marker or crayon
Scissors
Magazines
Glue

Teacher Preparation

1. Attach blue paper to the bulletin board.
2. Cut letters for the title "Into All the World" from construction paper, and glue them across the top of the blue paper.
3. Use a marker or crayon to draw a large circle in the center of the paper.
4. Cut two strips from construction paper, and glue them together for a cross. Cut and glue a triangle to each end of the cross to make arrows pointing out. (Older children can do steps 2-4 themselves.)
5. Provide magazines, scissors, and glue.

Classroom Activity

1. Talk about what the Great Commission means to our world today. To what distant people does the Gospel need to be spread today? To what people who live near us?
2. Tear or cut pictures of different kinds of people from magazines, and glue them in the circle.
3. Glue the cross with arrows in the center of the circle.

Other Ideas

1. Cut and glue pictures of different countries in the circle.
2. Cut the circle from construction paper.
3. Cut the circle from a piece of white paper, and divide it into sections. Give each child a section in which to draw people.
4. Cover the circle with twisted squares of green and blue tissue paper.

SS3824

ALPHABET PATTERNS

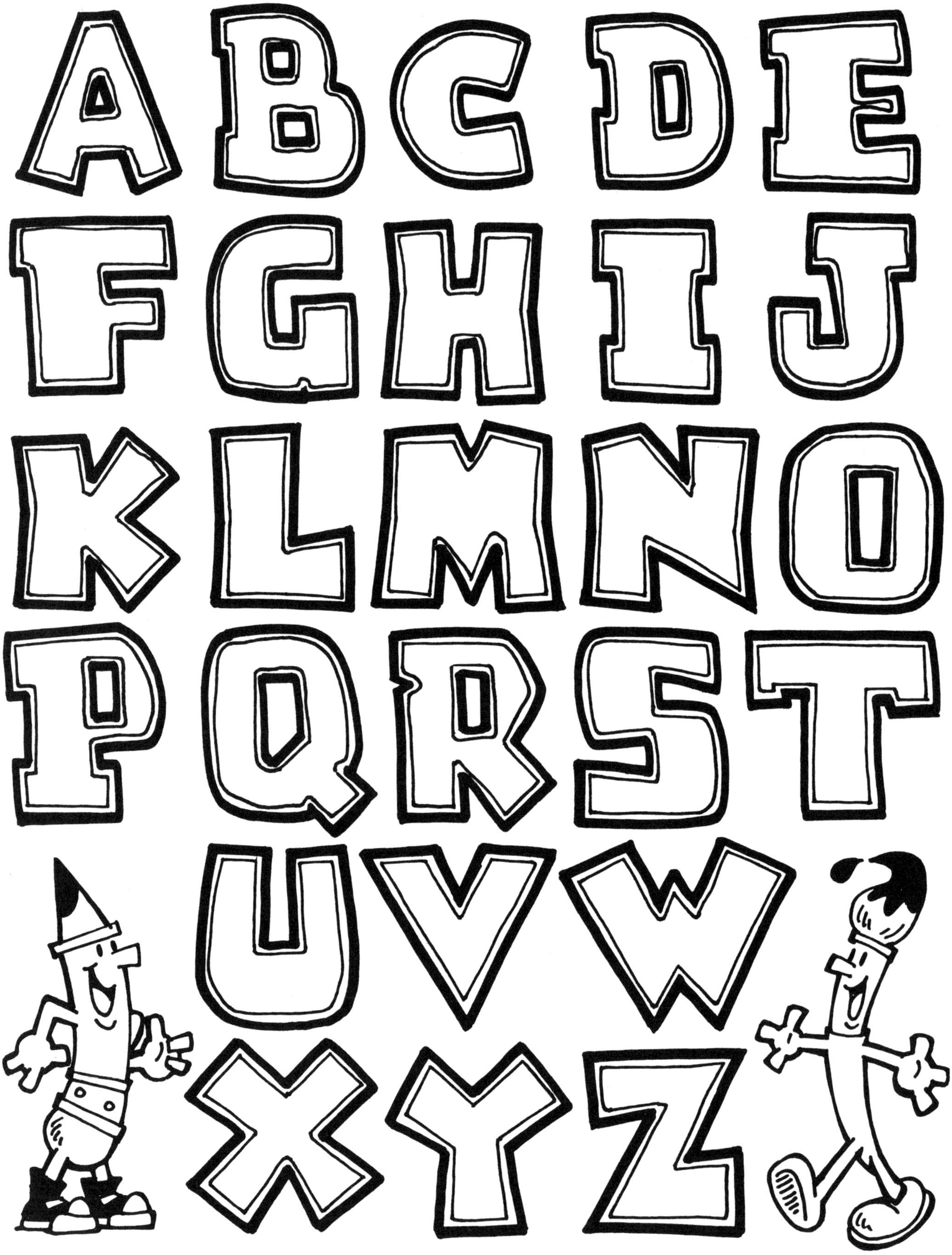

A B C D E
F G H I J
K L M N O
P Q R S T
U V W
X Y Z